**W9-CHI-560**

NECESSARY
IF MAILED
IN THE
UNITED STATES

# BUSINESS REPLY MAIL
FIRST CLASS    PERMIT NO. 2839   NEW YORK, NY

POSTAGE WILL BE PAID BY ADDRESSEE

### HUMAN SCIENCES PRESS, INC.
*72 FIFTH AVENUE*
*NEW YORK, N.Y. 10011-8004*        *(212) 243-6000*

I...IIII......II...II.I.I..IIII...II....I..I..I.I.II...II

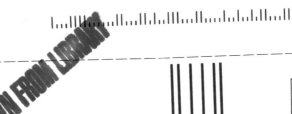

NO POSTAGE
NECESSARY
IF MAILED
IN THE
UNITED STATES

# BUSINESS REPLY MAIL
FIRST CLASS    PERMIT NO. 2839   NEW YORK, NY

POSTAGE WILL BE PAID BY ADDRESSEE

### HUMAN SCIENCES PRESS, INC.
*72 FIFTH AVENUE*
*NEW YORK, N.Y. 10011-8004*        *(212) 243-6000*

I...IIII......II...II.I.I..IIII...II....I..I..I.I.II...II

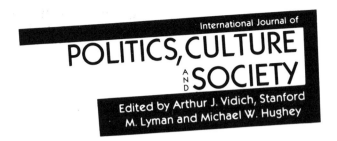

International Journal of

# POLITICS, CULTURE AND SOCIETY

## A Special Issue

# The SOCIOLOGY of CULTURE

## Edited by Arthur J. Vidich

**HUMAN SCIENCES PRESS, INC.**
72 FIFTH AVENUE
NEW YORK, N.Y. 10011-8004        (212) 243-6000

AAV 7238

ISBN—089885-396-6

Copyright 1987 by Human Sciences Press
72 Fifth Avenue
New York, New York 10011—8004

Printed in the United States of America

A Special Issue of the International Journal of Politics, Culture, and Society

Volume 1, Number 2                    Winter 1987

## The Sociology of Culture

**POLITICS, CULTURE, AND SOCIETY: AN INTERNATIONAL JOURNAL** provides a forum for discusion, dialogue, and debate on points of tension between state and civil society, between nations and global institutions. Its specific focus is the changing order of public and private spheres of life and the dialectic between rational organization and the emotional needs of human beings. Issues to be examined include: changing patterns in the coordination of societal and world economic and political institutions; new configurations of ethnic and racial groups and communities, class formations, emergent religions, personal networks, and special interests; articulations and social effects of mass culture, propaganda and the technoscientific breakthroughs in communication on classical culture and symbolic expression; and the consequences of contemporary social transformations for psyche, self, and kinship. The *Journal* is interdisciplinary and international in its orientation and scope and encourages historical and analytical essays and article length research monographs.

**MANUSCRIPTS** should be submitted in triplicate and typed double spaced throughout. References and citations should follow the American Psychological Association's style manual, 3rd edition. References should be listed alphabetically, not numbered in the order of their appearance in the article. Citations should not be footnoted but cited by the author(s) last name and year of publication. All correspondence concerning manuscripts should be sent to Arthur J. Vidich, c/o Department of Sociology, Graduate Faculty of the New School for Social Research, 65 Fifth Avenue, New York, NY 10003.

**SUBSCRIPTIONS** are on an academic year basis: $75.00 per volume for institutions and $32.00 for individuals. Prices slightly higher outside the U.S. **ADVERTISING** and subscription inquiries should be made to the business office: Human Sciences Press, 72 Fifth Avenue, New York, NY 10011-8004; (212) 243-6000.

**INDEXED AND ABSTRACTED IN:** Social Sciences Index, Current Contents, Sociological Abstracts, Book Review Editors' File, Sociology of Education Abstracts, Index to Periodical Literature on Aging, Social Work Research & Abstracts.

**PHOTOCOPYING:** Authorization to photocopy items for internal or personal use of specific clients is granted by Human Sciences Press for users registered with the Copyright Clearance Center (CCC) Transactional Reporting Service, provided that the base fee of $2.50 per copy, plus $.20 per page is paid directly to CCC, 27 Congress Street, Salem, MA 01970. For those organizations which have been granted a photocopy license from CCC, a separate system of payment has been arranged. The fee code for users of the Transactional Reporting Service is 0891-4486/87/$2.50+.20.

**POSTMASTER:** Send change of address and return journals if undeliverable to: Circulation, Human Sciences Press, 72 Fifth Avenue, New York, NY 10011-8004. Please return entire journal—do not remove cover.

ISSN 0891-4494    ISBN-089885-396-6    ICSOE 1 (2) 191-354 (1987)

# Editor's Note

Volume I, Number 2 of *Politics, Culture, and Society* focuses on the sociology of culture, including popular arts, museums, music, and publishing.

Our essays on the sociology of culture are written from historical and analytic perspectives and examine shifting connections of artistic and organizational subcultures to state and society. Some of these essays treat the dialectic of sacred and secular and the indeterminate boundaries between the two. Others open the discussion of the sociology of culture to meanings of nature reporting, the novel, music, film, and tourist art in Latin America, Greece, the United States, and Spain. Robert Lilienfeld critically examines the aesthetics of the music of Lukacs, Bloch, and Adorno from the perspectives of both musicology and social theory, and assesses the value of the Frankfurt School's sociology of music. Virtually every analysis of the many contours of modernity is in some way indebted to the work of Max Weber who examined the process of rationalization in numerous areas of social life, including that of music. Ferenc Feher assesses Adorno's and Bloch's writings on music from the perspective of Weber's sociology of music.

The editors of *Politics, Culture and Society* wish to thank the Moorhead State University Foundation, Moorhead State University, Minnesota, for a generous start-up grant enabling us to inaugurate Volume I of *Politics, Culture and Society*.

## In Memoriam

On May 2nd, 1987, Daria Cverna Martin, our Managing Editor and Colleague, was murdered in her Brooklyn home.

The senselessness of her death is a painful counterpoint to the meaningfulness of her life. To all that she did, Daria brought a strength of character and generosity of spirit that was founded on standards of human decency that she set for herself and which she expected from others. She refused to compromise those standards to the mindless demands of bureaucratic rigidity and in her day-to-day work exemplified a peculiarly modern and all-too-rare style of heroic humanity.

Daria was instrumental in the formation of this journal and its purpose. Her death underscores our own efforts to wrest some meaning, however limited, from an arbitrary world. The journal will bear as its legacy some of the meaning she gave to our lives.

# Artworks As Symbols In International Politics

## Judith Huggins Balfe

The use of artworks as symbolic carriers, as mediators of politics and as propaganda for secular and religious ideologies (including, of course, the "aesthetic religion" of "art-for-art's-sake") is an old phenomenon. The Sphinx and the Pyramids, for example, symbolized pharaonic power to the Egyptian populace. But it took the imperialism of Alexander and his Roman successors to carry about, import, and install artworks in new contexts to symbolize political power to other than the original audience—i.e., to recognize their ability to transcend socio-cultural limits and stand as "universal symbols." This is quite different than destroying "pagan idols" of the conquered "heathen." Rather, it is a recognition that the aesthetic power of artworks, however it may be defined, transcends their creators by enhancing the identification of the audience with that power. So too, the status of the artworks' sponsor, in a halo effect, is enhanced in the eyes of that audience. If the artworks are of universal significance, speaking across cultural boundaries, so is their discerning patron or owner. That, at least, is the claim.

This claim is more difficult to sustain with respect to the performing arts, where the idiosyncrasies of the interpreting performer are not altogether subject to the patron's control and, in any case, are not regarded as being "owned." By contrast, such a claim is more acceptable with respect to the visual arts, because the artist's creativity is embodied in a fixed object. In this case, possession is equivalent to control, although, given the perspectival idiosyncrasies of any audience, even here the presentation of the artwork must be carefully orchestrated if the patron is to reap the benefits of the desired "halo."

Such orchestration has become more complicated and more necessary in recent years as the world's great artworks have been increasingly used in the competition between various "imperialistic" powers and assigned various roles in international propaganda. The variety of these roles, and the reasons why artworks are considered to be politically useful, are evident in the following comments:

The International Journal of Politics, Culture and Society, 1(2), Winter 1987

Art can take a person and open him up in a way you couldn't any other way.

> Norton Simon, industrialist
> and art collector, 1972

A visitor who has spent some hours admiring masterworks from a foreign collection is unlikely to have his political views significantly altered . . . (but) if the visitor acquires in the process a better understanding of the culture which produces the art, and of the people who now treasure it, that . . . has political value for the U.S.

> Peter Solmssen, Advisor on the Arts,
> U.S. State Department, 1976

At its highest, art has an integrity that sets it apart from the unending give and take of politics.

> Walter Goodman, editor,
> *The New York Times*, 1977

Culture has no connection with transitory political events.

> Leo Castelli, art dealer, 1977

(There is an) essential quality of art as a unifier of mankind.

> Teddy Kollek, Mayor of Jerusalem, 1982

(Cancellation of an exhibition of archeological artifacts from the West Bank) reinforces efforts to delegitimize the State of Israel.

> Morris Abram, former U. S. Representative
> to the U.N. Commission on Human Rights,
> 1982

Museum officials are beginning to wonder about the price we may be paying for seeing these (masterpieces). They are asking what advantage, if any, we are deriving from their display here.

> Hilton Kramer, art critic,
> *The New York Times*, 1975

Most of these comments agree that great art is above politics, and as a result it works politically because it moves individuals to levels of universal understanding! But as others suggest, such attempts to move the audience are often recognized to have ideological motivations. In such cases, is the art itself diminished by its presentation? If the "halo" is seen to be tarnished, is its source dimmed as well? How can we begin to disentangle this issue, to understand the use of artworks as symbols in international politics and propaganda which work only if they do in fact transcend their political mission (Balfe, 1985a; 1985b)?

I will here be considering visual artworks, sent on cultural exchanges to the United States from several foreign nations during the last 20 years, to illuminate their varying aesthetic and political roles and thereby respond to the issues just raised. Some of these art exchanges were in "blockbuster" exhibitions which toured American museums; others, sent at different times by the same foreign states, were of appeal largely to sophisticated elites and not to the mass public. Four "variables" will be considered here on a case by case basis, to demonstrate their interaction. Firstly, variations in the obvious political agenda of the sponsoring state are related to variations, secondly, in the aesthetic qualities and power of the artworks themselves (whether subtle or obvious) and, thirdly, in the elite or mass characteristics of the intended audience. Finally, the "received" interpretation of the exhibited works as constructed in accompanying catalogues, labels, critical reviews and wider press coverage, has varied as well.

To be sure, the host museums have had their own non-political agendas, which have made them particularly receptive to accepting state-sponsored loan exhibitions, and museum directors and curators have often been instrumental in helping to arrange such exchanges. Loan exhibitions of high quality, on only temporary display, have proven almost necessary to attract the audiences whose numbers have come to serve as the yardstick by which to measure museum success and even a city's "cultural quotient."

However, not all such exhibitions need be blockbusters to attract the multitudes. A smaller exhibition of superb works can be an equal *success d'estime* among critical and powerful elites, even if the attendance is also smaller. Still, favorable press coverage is crucial in both cases, for the mass audience must be informed that the artwork-ambassadors are present, even if the masses are not invited to attend their reception. Hence, the examples of press coverage provided here are almost entirely from *The New York Times*, the newspaper *par excellence* of the educated, cosmopolitan classes—including the traditional suburban elites as well as the new urban "yuppies," both of whom identify with art and culture as evidence of their social status, but who often lack independent criteria of taste with which to guide their cultural choices (Bensman & Vidich, 1971; Kramer, 1982). As a result, they are all the more dependent upon the *Times* critics to tell them the cultural and political significance of artworld events, whether or not they attend them in person. Accordingly, *Times* coverage becomes an important aspect of the political uses of the arts, for its interpretations provide and describe evidence of artworks either as propaganda or "merely" as art.

It must be recognized at the outset that the museum blockbuster, as a type of exhibition or as a factor in museum success, is not just a product of Cold War and more recent political and economic strains. Indeed, the phenomenon is at least 50 years old. In 1932, for instance, "Whistler's Mother" traveled from the Louvre to the Chicago World's Fair, and was also displayed at museums in St. Louis, Cleveland, Boston, and at the Museum of Modern Art in New York. While it is owned by France, its presence here reasserted its American identity. For most Americans, it is as symbolic of national culture and pride as Gilbert Stuart's portrait of George Washington, and carries equal emotional weight. Thus during the Depression, when few had either the financial or intellectual resources to be interested in art or museums, over 2 million people made the effort to see "Whistler's Mother" while the painting was in the United States.

Such a popular response was not always expected or welcomed by museums during this period. An exhibition of the works of Van Gogh, which was organized by the Museum of Modern Art in 1935 and traveled to Detroit, Cleveland, Chicago, Philadelphia, and Boston, attracted overflow crowds everywhere and, in turn, irritated the museum curators who had not anticipated such a reaction from a previously unresponsive mass audience. Once this potential audience was recognized, however, it was increasingly catered to. Immediately after World War II, traveling exhibitions of European Old Masters were arranged through the Metropolitan Museum as an expression of gratitude to Americans by the people—and the museums—of Holland, England, France, and specifically Berlin and Vienna for the safe return of their treasures from their wartime hiding places. Attendance at all of the American host museums for these various exhibitions doubled that of the preceding years. Obviously, millions of Americans responded to the common appeal made in all of these shows, as they had to the "native motherhood" aura of "Whistler's Mother" and the intense individuality of Van Gogh. Now, however, the "message" of the Old Masters, of European origin but at least temporarily of American soil, was the unity of mankind and the triumph of Western civilization over economic, political, and military conflicts and competition. As such, these exhibitions of blockbuster proportions legitimated the formal organization of the wartime Allies under NATO, and the founding of the United Nations. Granted such evident successes, it is not surprising that art was increasingly thought capable in some small but vital measure of healing the residual bitterness and the wounds of war.

## Japanese Art and American Audiences

While American hostility toward the Germans and Italians seemed to give way fairly readily, animosity toward the Japanese was compounded by the traditional racial discrimination toward Asians, especially on the West Coast, and by the guilt felt by the more sensitive as a result of the wartime incarceration of Japanese-American citizens, the appropriation of their properties, and the destruction caused by the atomic bomb. Combining this residue of wartime animosity and guilt, the general incomprehensibility of the Asian mind and culture to the West, and the fact that Japan had also since become our political ally, it is no wonder that art was again pressed into diplomatic service to speak to the sensitive and, hopefully, to reach the insensitive as well.

Thus, in 1953 (presumably with the assistance of the U.S. State Department), the Japanese government sponsored a large exhibit of their classical art as a good will gesture to the United States. After opening in the nation's capital, it traveled to Seattle, Chicago and Boston. In order to monitor and evaluate its success in affecting the political attitudes of its American audiences, a team of social scientists conducted a study under the sponsorship of the Japan Society to assess the audience response. It is the only such instance I have been able to find of an adequate study of the impact of any such exhibition upon the political attitudes of the audience. As such, and because its findings underlie the distinction made above between elite and mass audiences as an important variable in any analysis of the political efficacy of art, it is worth recounting the study in some detail.

The authors, Bower and Sharpe (1956), distributed 6500 questionnaires to audience members before and after they attended the show, and conducted interviews with some 700 visitors in Seattle, Chicago and Boston. Generally, audience response varied according to city, as did the publicity which surrounded the exhibition. In Seattle, it was considered "a public event of great importance." The city had never before hosted such a major international exhibition. Moreover, like other West Coast cities, Seattle had a long history of prejudice toward Japanese. In any case, publicized as having more-than-artistic importance, the exhibition attracted a mass audience of 73,000—one out of every seven Seattle adults. In Chicago and Boston, however, both cities being more frequently on the circuit for traveling art shows and also both having less traditional animosity toward (and a smaller population of) the Japanese, the exhibition was publicized, respectively, as "a major exhibit" and as "just another art show." Hence it was described as being of interest primarily to the already educated museum-goer and art-lover, i.e., the elite audience. Accordingly, it attracted only one out of every 67 adults in Chicago and one out of every 82 in Boston. Here, then, is a test case for the argument that the same artworks can affect the attitudes of elite and mass audiences alike.

In fact, the mass audience in Seattle remained largely uncomprehending or disappointed. A full third said that they had learned nothing about the Japanese, while another fifth came away with unfavorable ideas. In contrast, the elite audiences of Chicago and Boston had more positive responses, and reported learning more—but they already had attitudes favorable to the Japanese which had motivated them to attend in the first place. In sum, both the aesthetic and political "good will" purpose of the exhibition failed for the masses attracted by what we now call "blockbuster hype" to a "media event." The aesthetic ends were successfully served for elite audiences, but even here, any political impact was nil. Regardless of audience type, the exhibition primarily reinforced previously held attitudes toward the Japanese.

Given this expensive and rather negative finding, it is no wonder that successive international exhibitions have not been comparably studied (even as their economic impacts are examined in great detail). Still, the finding demonstrated all too clearly that if propagandistic intentions are to be realized through art exhibitions, greater efforts would be needed to anticipate the possibly indeterminate and differing responses of different audiences, and hence to control for effect in the planning of any future art exchanges, whether targeted at elite or mass audiences.

Indeed, it was already apparent that those planning such exhibitions needed to consider the reactions of the official sponsors as well. The United States had begun to send American artworks abroad as cultural emissaries during World War II, when Nelson Rockefeller, under the auspices of the State Department, sent American works from the Museum of Modern Art collections on tour of Latin America. The purpose was to persuade Latin American elites—both intellectuals and aristocrats—of the substantive quality of North American culture, and thus to solidify their loyalty to the anti-Fascist Allies. A few years later, as the Cold War polarized international politics anew, the State Department again sent works by contemporary American artists on tour of Europe. But because the works selected were "modern" in the first such instance, and Abstract Expressionist in the second, both exhibitions were attacked by American Congressmen as being anti-American and even Communist (as, indeed, some of the *artists* had been in the 30's). At the same time, the rationale for the selection of these works was to demonstrate that freedom of expression was fostered by American capitalism (Cockcroft, 1974; Guilbault, 1984; Larson, 1983). Obviously, some symbolic significance was attached to these exhibitions by their American sponsors. They were either "Communist" or "anti-Communist" according to the aesthetic and political ideology of the individual observer, regardless of what the artists themselves intended in their works. As for their interpretations by the targeted audiences of Latin American and European elites, there is some evidence that American claims to a culture which fostered creative freedom were widely believed. (This would seem to be the main reason for the resentment of such leftist critics as Cockcroft and Guilbault at their use in this fashion: as propaganda, they worked! As a result, rightwing critics in Congress no longer protested that use, and the domestic controversy surrounding the use of art as American propaganda declined.)

In any event, by the mid-50's, with the experience of the foreign success of exhibitions of American modern art and the mixed success of the exhibition of Japanese art in the United States, the techniques of presenting artworks to support political agendas had become increasingly refined. And as these techniques became more widely understood, in turn they were more widely practiced.

## The Institutionalization of Blockbuster Exhibitions

Among the first indications of the potential size of the national mass audience was the response to the 1961 exhibition by the Metropolitan Museum of Art of its newly purchased Rembrandt, "Aristotle Contemplating the Bust of Homer." Then the most expensive painting ever acquired, with a price tag of over $2 million, it attracted an audience of over a million people in its first few months on display. Its popularity was outdone by the 1962 loan from the Louvre of the "Mona Lisa," arranged through French Cultural Minister Andre' Malraux (who provided Charles de Gaulle with daily reports of the size of the attending crowds [Meyer, 1979]). And even this popularity was outdone by Michelangelo's "Pieta," loaned by the Vatican to the New York World's Fair in 1965. These successes demonstrated the ability of a simple "theme"—even a single "world class" artwork—to symbolize the transcendence of the sponsor and, in turn, the exhibitor. The symbiosis benefited everyone: the sponsor (e.g., de Gaulle and France, or the Pope and the Vatican) was seen as beneficent; the host (e.g., the Metropolitan Museum or National Gallery, or just New York City) attracted new crowds and favorable publicity; and the mass audience was "blessed" by coming into the presence of sublime art, acquiring some increased cultural status as well among others unable to so attend.

Certainly this coalition of individual and institutional agendas can be seen to work even without the inclusion of political propaganda as one party to the coalition. For example, in 1967, new director Thomas Hoving proclaimed the Metropolitan Museum as the premier museum in the world by inaugurating his tenure with a blockbuster exhibition from the Met's own collections, "In the Presence of Kings." Each work was selected because it had been associated with or commissioned by royalty; each work was, not incidentally, superb. The show, as well, was an "unintentional (?) recapitulation of the Museum's prime donors" who had collected and given the works in the first place (Lerman, 1970, p. 287). Thus demonstrated once again was the elective affinity of the power and wealth of the sponsors, the power and beauty of the works and, presumably, the virtue of all concerned, including members of the mass audience. Given the key ingredients of obvious and overwhelming power of the artworks, the formula for The Blockbuster, for propaganda purposes, had been established.

### Fund-Raising and Political Legitimation: The Case of "Tut"

Just after the visit of the "Mona Lisa," in 1963 Egypt sent some 36 objects from Tutankhamen's tomb on a Smithsonian-sponsored nationwide tour. The specifically articulated agenda was to raise money for the relocation of Abu Simbel, scheduled to be flooded by the rising waters behind the Aswan Dam. It is instructive to compare this exhibition with the much more widely heralded blockbuster Tut show of 1976-9 in terms of the aesthetic quality of the works included, the intended audience, and the political nature of the sponsor's agenda. At the time of the earlier Tut show, I was working at the Museum of Fine Arts in Boston, which was one of its hosts. Even then I was struck by the low-key publicity, designed either for typical museum "culture vultures" or for school groups in the age brackets exposed to Ancient Civilization in the Massachusetts curriculum. There was some wider press coverage of the artworks included, most of them gold and all subtle in detail and precious in size, but the interpretive material both inside and outside the museum was utterly scholarly. Here was no "romance" of a "curse of the mummy's tomb," but rather a fairly dry discussion for a self-selected audience of art historians and connoisseurs. Not surprisingly (as had been the case with the comparably delicate artworks included in the Japanese show of 1953, discussed above), in Boston this first Tut exhibition attracted few of the "masses" other than school children who were bussed in for the event, and the overall attendance of 60,000 was only half that which had been attracted the previous year to another Van Gogh show at the museum.

Contrast this with the later blockbuster exhibition, which had 55 larger and more impressive objects, a much higher total price tag (which itself became part of the publicity and the media event which the exhibition was intended to be), a much larger mass audience and, of course, the much more politicized atmosphere of the time. It was no accident that the Egyptians agreed to send these priceless and irreplaceable works at the time when Sadat was negotiating the Camp David accords and the American public was to be weaned away from the notion that Arabs in general and Egyptians in particular were less civilized than Israelis. Full press coverage of the finances involved carried the latent message that the Egyptians were participants in the Western economic order and accepted its capitalistic ethos; more overtly, with scholarly disclaimers that there could be any political agenda behind this exhibition, the Egyptians were depicted as the founders of Western civilization. Lest this seem the only latent political message, the exhibition also celebrated the romance of British (imperialistic) archeology. Thus by publicizing their primacy in discovery, Sadat symbolically reached an accord with the British as well.

Obviously, compared to the earlier Tut exhibition, the later one was much greater in scale on all four of the variables I listed at outset: the aesthetic power and overwhelming quality of the artworks; the size of the intended audience; the complexity and importance of the political agenda; and the public interpretation of it all by the media. If the works had been less powerful, merely as elegant and subtle as in the first exhibition, they would have been less able to live up to the hype which attracted the ignorant and the insensitive—as had happened in Seattle with the 1953 Japanese show. And in turn, much of the economic and political effects would have been diminished. Certainly the 8 million in audience and $16 million in world-wide profit would have been lower.

In addition, the staging of the second Tut show was enhanced in scale. Not only was big business involved in various commercial spin-offs—granted (or not) "official" imprimature by the museums which accepted and sold various items of "Tut-mania" at the shows which, in turn, contribute ever increasing monies to the always-strained museum budgets—but a team of Smithsonian observers traveled with the show, building expertise on crowd control from one site to the next; Ticketron handled the national distribution of admission slots; host cities calculated profits to such ancillary institutions as restaurants just as host museums gleefully added up their own profits (e.g., $1.5 million to the Seattle museum). In sum, status legitimation was practiced, and practicable, from the level of the individual member of the audience who participated in this media event, to the art museum which hosted it, to the national states involved.

## Art Exhibitions and Détente with China

For a comparable pair of examples, let us look at two loan shows from China. In 1971, acting as front man to negotiate Richard Nixon's 1972 visit to Peking and the formal state recognition that was to follow, Henry Kissinger proposed that the Chinese send some of their ancient art on an international tour. Accordingly in 1973 and 74, an exhibit insured for over $50 million visited Paris, London, Toronto, and Washington—with an additional stop in Kansas City scheduled as an after-thought, to reach the American "heartland." The exhibit consisted of 400 works, all excavated by Chinese archeologists since the Communists had come to power. Although of obviously ancient lineage, these works were to be seen as "products" of Mao's revolution.

American press coverage started when the exhibition opened in Paris to "thrilled crowds" (*The New York Times,* May 9, 1973), continued in London ("attendance was 750,000") and increased when the show reached Toronto. In the words of *Times* critic John Russell, "It will give many thousands of people a new idea of the present regime in China . . ." (Oct. 9, 1974). Once in Washington, the exhibition was hailed as "stunning," and only an occasional critic demurred by noting the overtly "propagandistic" nature of the explicit layout of the exhibition according to Marxist theories and categories of historical development (*The New York Times,* Aug. 25, 1974). Paradoxically, despite the overt diplomacy involved in this show, it was not hyped to the fullest extent, perhaps because the real connoisseurs who were asked to review the exhibition saw through the propaganda (even if most were too tactful to complain about it). Additionally, the works themselves were not all of superb quality, whether measured according to subtle or overwhelming impact. Although there were long lines to see the exhibit in Washington and Kansas City, unlike the Tut show, attendance figures in the United States were never reported in *The Times.*

Following the downfall of the Gang of Four in 1976, various Chinese bans on Western culture were lifted and artists and artworks from America were granted cautious permission to visit China. In 1979, the United States gave formal recognition to mainland China, and Deng himself visited this country. With cultural exchanges becoming increasingly common and with increasing critical dismay at the politicizing of international "détente" exhibitions, attempts to create media events, blockbusters, and appeals to the mass audience were held in check. Following Deng's visit, a second U.S. tour of Chinese art was arranged, but with political and cultural relations between the two states now well established, a lower profile was possible for art. This exhibit was of interest primarily to elite audiences and was reported as such. While *Times* critic Hilton Kramer was impressed with some of the Bronze Age works included, notably several life-size terra cotta funerary figures of warriors and ritual bronze vessels, he also warned the novice that this exhibition was "not altogether easy for a public uninstructed in the rudiments of Chinese archeology" (*The New York Times,* April 11, 1980)—a warning no one even thought of making about the Tut exhibition.

In other words, given a lower political agenda, this exhibition could consist of works of subtle qualities (i.e. ritual bronzes), scholarly labels and accompanying catalog, and direct its audience appeal almost exclusively to elites. No Ticketron sales were necessary.

## The Rationalization of Art—As—Propaganda

Before turning to a third example, that of exchanges with the Soviet Union, it is first necessary to note the increasingly overt involvement of the U.S. State Department and other governmental agencies in such exhibitions. (At the same time, the amount of such involvement must not be overstated: the National Endowment for the Arts and various "arts diplomacy" programs, even now, are funded at a lower figure than are military bands in the overall defense budget.) In 1974 the State Department created the new position of Arts Advisor, which was filled by Peter Solmssen, a former Foreign Service officer and lawyer who had already helped the Met Museum's Thomas Hoving begin to arrange the details for the Tut exhibit that opened in 1976. In 1975, Congress passed a bill whereby the federal government agreed to cover up to $50 million in insurance costs per show for exchange exhibitions certified by the State Department to be in the national interest. Such coverage enabled artwork tours to continue, as the host museums could no longer afford the escalating insurance fees, but it also relegated power of purse and permission to the state, rather than retaining it in the international art historical and museum community.

Additionally, the expanding National Endowment for the Humanities had helped to fund U.S. exhibition costs for a number of international art exchanges, including the Tut tour and the 1973–4 Chinese show. Obviously, such government sponsorship provided political legitimation of the United States as a patron of culture, just as it validated both the artworks themselves as having supra-political, universal aesthetic significance, and the interpretation of those works provided by their sponsors. (As noted, in the 1973 Chinese show, this version was strictly according to Marx.) Clearly, as some critics increasingly warned (Kramer, 1975), the American context for such shows was becoming more and more politicized.

The trend had become clear even prior to these changes in State Department activity and the critical dismay they provoked. Just as Nixon's meeting with the Chinese in 1972 had led to cultural exchanges, so too did his dealings with the Soviets.[1] In 1973, he and Brezhnev signed cultural accords, which were affirmed at the 1974 summit meeting. But with the institutional mechanisms not yet in place for direct American governmental sponsorship (the insurance guarantees had not yet passed through Congress), the first two Soviet loan exhibitions were arranged and funded by Armand Hammer. In 1973 and again in 1975, major works from the Hermitage collections of Impressionist and Old Master paintings came to the U.S. via Hammer's intercession. Hammer was hardly a disinterested third party.[2] Indeed, his participation in these exchanges in turn legitimated his own major institutional properties. One, Occidental Petroleum (purchased in 1957 and by this time, suspect for its involvements in Libya), provided exhibition funding as a tax write-off. A second Hammer property, Knoedler's Art Gallery in New York, garnered the same benefit by providing housing for both of these loan shows, and reaped enhanced publicity as a source for Old Masters when the exhibitions went on nationwide tour to many other cities. More obviously, the exhibitions proclaimed the message that the Soviet state, which owned the works, was civilized and utterly appreciative of Western culture.

For more sophisticated viewers, of course, ownership is not automatically testimony to artistic sensitivity. Thus, in 1975 the Soviets allowed the Met Museum to exhibit Scythian gold objects which had never before left the U.S.S.R. Here, comparable to the then-anticipated Tut show, the message was that sumptuous and remarkably sophisticated work was created by ancestors of contemporary Soviet peoples, who were thus obviously descended from "cultured stock" and not to be considered "barbaric." At the same time, the implicit claim was made that current Soviet culture could be depoliticized because it was now universalized on art-historical grounds.

In exchange for the Scythian works, some 100 Met-owned paintings (all of them realistic, by Soviet choice) were sent to Leningrad and Moscow. Russian response to this exhibition received scant attention in the American press, and those permitted to attend were, in any case, members of the Soviet elite. In contrast to this seemingly deliberately low American profile in its first loan exhibition to the U.S.S.R., the Russian exhibitions for the United States just discussed were designed as blockbusters, with magnificent works which could appeal to elite as well as to mass audiences. They were widely publicized both as "apolitical" art having historical significance, and as having inherently political importance for their very "apoliticality!" In these paradoxical claims, no one could escape the underlying message of détente. So nicely was all of this proceeding that, with State Department cooperation, Hoving announced with much fanfare five future blockbuster shows to come to the Met from Soviet museums.

Then came the fraying of détente and, with the politicization of art, the disruption of any remaining "art-for-art's-sake" ethos. Indeed, the artworld itself became politically activist. In 1976, the opening in Paris of an explicitly labeled "Anti-Soviet Art Exhibition" received widespread coverage in the United States. In this show, Soviet emigré artists protested the détente-like presence in Paris of the Moscow Circus and the Moiseyev Ballet. Within months, even more American press attention was given to Soviet suppression of contemporary artists. Two of them, Komar and Melamid, became "household words" in the artworld before they were allowed to emigrate to Israel (where they have since disappeared into relative obscurity so far as the American artworld or political press are concerned). Obviously, various sides could take advantage of the increasingly politicized international art exhibition scene, and indeed, the major theme of the 1977 Venice Biennale was "The Art of Dissent."

In this context of overt propagandizing, even an "art-for-art's sake" purist view was interpreted as a political statement. More to the point of our current discussion, the concurrent Soviet-American détente shows led to contempt rather than to applause. While the Met sent another show of American realism to Russia (this time insisting on including works by Andy Warhol and Jasper Johns as evidence of American artistic freedom—works which evidently met with near-total incomprehension), an overly-billed "Détente Show" of Russian and Soviet paintings opened in New York at the Met. Like the selection of Met-owned paintings for the Russians, this collection was comparably limited to works chosen to comply with cultural self-definitions and official political policies. This meant, of course, that the show featured works of Socialist Realism rather than Pop Art or other avant garde abstractions. Not surprisingly, given the notorious lack of aesthetic value in most official Socialist Realism, the "Détente Show" was widely panned as "dismal" (Kramer, 1977). If elite Soviet audiences could see no social merit in Warhol, even unknowledgeable American audiences could see no artistic merit in these Russian works—all the more when told by critics like Kramer that there was none. Attendance at the exhibiton was therefore unimpressive, and the Metropolitan Museum itself lost lustre for hanging such overt propaganda with no redeeming aesthetic virtues.

But if, in this show, the Soviet propaganda message was lost through its own transparency (Balfe, 1985b) and through its publicized suppression of even mediocre artists, the commissars of culture seemed to recognize their error. For the next two years, in successive loan shows to the United States, they followed the newly reasserted international etiquette for cultural exchanges in such a politically-charged atmosphere: "I won't talk politics if you won't." (This, too, becomes a political decision.) Thus, in 1979, the Met showed "Treasures of the Kremlin", heralded as "the crown jewels" demonstrating "Moscow's early sense of a demanding spiritual destiny" (The New York Times, May 13, 1979). At the same time, books such as The Art of the October Revolution and museum exhibitions of Russian Formalist and Constructivist avant garde works (at the Pompidou Center in Paris in a "Paris-Moscow" exhibition given wide American coverage and, in the United States, other shows at the Guggenheim, Los Angeles County, and Hirschhorn museums) celebrated the extraordinary vitality of artists committed to the revolutionary movement in 1917. Little was said in catalog or other interpretive material about their subsequent fate following the triumph of Socialist Realism under Stalin. To be sure, all of these shows required both Soviet cooperation and tact on the part of the hosts to ensure that "embarrassing" political matters were not mentioned. The purity of aesthetics was reasserted as primary.

In 1980, however, the Soviet Union invaded Afghanistan. Once again, politics and propaganda came first, and already-arranged exchanges of artworks were abruptly cancelled along with American participation in the Olympic Games to be held in Moscow. Almost ready to be shipped to the United States was the largest exhibition of works from the Hermitage ever to leave Russia, an exhibition upon which Control Data Corporation had already spent $1 million in preliminary plans and materials (as part of a deal to sell computers to the Soviets). All it took was State Department refusal to justify federal insurance coverage on grounds of state interest, and the exhibition did not move. While cancellation of the exhibit by Washington officials doubtless would have occurred in any case, along with cancellation of the general cultural exchange accords, in this case strong grass roots opposition to the show became evident even before any official decisions. Members of the National Guard, which operates the Armory at which the show would have been housed in New York, had already denied its exhibition there out of patriotic belief that to allow it would be to condone and legitimate Soviet actions in Afghanistan. As they saw it, the Russians would profit financially from the exchange (through sales of replicas, post cards, etc.) as well as reaping political profits. But both possibilities could be raised only because the aesthetic qualities and superiority of these Hermitage-owned works were generally recognized, as was the potential popularity of the show and its ability to transcend social and political contexts. Otherwise, as with the earlier "Détente Show," the audience would have seen the propaganda message too easily.

Intimations of a change in mood began to appear in 1984, when *The New York Times* published an Op-Ed piece by Igor Moiseyev, director of the U.S.S.R. Dance Ensemble, advocating a renewal of cultural exchanges. He concluded that "official America" was to blame for their cessation. (Feb. 18, 1984). Two months later *The Times* covered a privately-sponsored performance by Soviet musicians at the Whitney Museum of Art in New York, and quoted its leader as stating that "art is international by its very essence. The more people shake hands, the less they'll point rifles" (April 4, 1984). But it was not until the summit conference between Ronald Reagan and Mikhail Gorbachev in December 1985 that a new cultural exchange between the two powers became official. Once again, Armand Hammer was involved as facilitator and benefi-ciary: not only was Occidental Petroleum to be corporate sponsor for an exhibition of 40 Soviet-owned Impressionist paintings in three American cities, but in exchange, 40 works from Hammer's own extensive collection (along with others from the National Gallery) were to be displayed in Soviet museums, all again insured against damage or seizure by the American government (*The New York Times,* Dec. 14, 1985).

It is obvious from this history that when major powers undertake subsidy and sponsorship of art exhibitions, whether designed as blockbusters or not, changes in international affairs will determine whether the art is exchanged at all. Less obviously, the public gets caught up in the politicized "frame" put on the art, and willy-nilly compounds any aesthetic response to it with a reaction to its more-or-less obvious propagandistic purposes. Given both the general insecurity of most people on matters of aesthetic judgment, and their reliance on the critical reviews of the *cognoscenti*, any authentic artwork-to-viewer interaction is even further undermined. All the greater is the contradiction between the supposed universal-

yet-individualizing values of the art and the instrumental values
of its use as propaganda.


## Religion, Art, and the Universal Church

Let us consider a final example of international politics conducted
through museum exhibition and collection of artworks. This time
the "competing" state is the Vatican, and the issue at stake is
monopolization of the symbols of redemption, either through the
Universal Church or through the secularized "salvation" provided
by either art, science, or politics.

In 1973, Pope Paul VI opened a new Vatican gallery of modern
art, not limited to religious art *per se* but including works
representing "a religious reference, intention, or subject, freely
conceived by the artist" (*The New York Times,* June 24, 1973).
Over 600 of the works to be collected were by Americans, specifically
because there was then no permanent center of American art in
Europe. Since 4 million visitors attend the Vatican museums yearly,
the Pope was not only asserting to a vast public the Papacy's
participation in the pluralistic, contemporary world, but he was
becoming in effect, European spokesman for American culture on
grounds supposedly above the political rivalries that were even
then affecting artworld exchanges.

A decade and two popes later, and after four years of negotiations
and preparations, the "Art of the Papacy" came to America in
what was billed as "the most expensive ever" blockbuster, to be
shown at the Metropolitan Museum in New York, and also in
Chicago and San Francisco. Not including insurance, the
exhibition was budgeted at $8 million, a figure much noted in the
advance publicity. In New York alone it drew an audience of
800,000, two thirds that which had attended the Tut blockbuster.
Indeed, half of the New York audience was non-Catholic, and only
20% were noted in follow-up polls to have been disappointed by
it.

Some of the 237 works included in the show were of world reknown
(e.g., the "Apollo Belvedere"); other objects were of lesser aesthetic
or art historical importance even as they spanned the Ancient
World and the two millenia of Christianity. The exhibition
concluded with works from the Vatican's modern museum and
works by tribal peoples of Africa and Oceania. It is important to

note that the exhibition was arranged chronologically, not in terms of the creation of the works but rather in terms of the periods in which they were collected by the various popes. As stated by the director of the Vatican collections: "For the first time these works have a different message. Alone, they always have the language of beauty. Altogether, they speak of the history of the Vatican Museum and the Popes" (*The New York Times Magazine,* Jan. 16, 1983). The issue was not that the artworks themselves were (and are) of universal significance, transcending their socio-historical origins through sheer beauty. Rather, it was the sensibility and taste of the Papacy which was making this claim to universality and "pluralistic" respect for all mankind. As with every other blockbuster, however, its claims could be accepted only if the artworks themselves were of superlative quality.

Certainly many of the works were "world class." But even so, and despite critical support from the press, the modern works selected for the exhibition were "underwhelming." The tribal works, moreover, had clearly been collected less from an appreciation for their power as artworks than from a recognition that left *in situ,* they would have retained their place in the native religions which Catholic missionaries were trying to uproot. As with the détente exhibitions of Chinese or Soviet works, public interpretations of the Vatican show were conducted with diplomatic tact and for comparable reasons.

A correlation appears to exist between this exhibition and the increasing political activism of the present Pope and the American bishops. Given its inclusion of non-Christian works and its setting in a secular "art-for-art's sake" museum context, this exhibition legitimated the Papal claim to be considered a power in the secular as well as the religious world—indeed, that in the propaganda wars of the modern age, the Papacy has legions of its own. Who could have been surprised when subsequently the United States formally recognized the Vatican as a political state?

A number of other examples could be discussed here, notably the Greek-sponsored exhibitions of Aegean Art and "The Search for Alexander," the latter of which opened in London at the time of Greek entry into the Common Market, and pressure on England for the return of the Elgin Marbles. Most recently exhibitions and performances involved in "The Festival of India" throughout America, and the Washington-only exhibition of collections from "Treasure Houses of Britain" have demonstrated that even allied states may attempt to cement mutual loyalties through the mechanism of museum blockbusters.[3] When sent on international tours for purposes of universal aesthetic enrichment, the artworks of even friendly states also carry political "halos" to audiences who have long since come to expect such frames and respond accordingly.

## Summary and Conclusion

Certainly, in the contemporary international scene which places few economic and political limits on tourism by elites and which includes an educationally broadened awareness of cultural similarities of peoples, it would not seem necessary to subject fragile and irreplaceable artworks to the risk of permanent damage and even destruction by shipping them around the world. Instead, those who dominate political and economic institutions could simply visit the works where they are; others could do so vicariously through film and television coverage. Nonetheless, as these examples have attested, artworks are increasingly sent traveling to help to "normalize" political relations, as bona fides of trust precisely because of their fragility and pricelessness—as in an exchange of hostages, or, in tribal societies, of women. Accordingly, the artworks are intended to "win the hearts and minds of the people," especially those who are not in the international tourist set and who may never even attend their domestic exhibition but know of it only through media coverage. In such supposedly improved and less suspicious environments, more formal diplomatic, political, economic and military alliances can be negotiated with less resistance from local, antagonistic constituencies.

Ownership and, by implication, sensitive appreciation of great artworks have long been taken as symbolic of superior ethical and moral qualities, of "higher"culture generally. To be sure, such claims may be more persuasive when made by living artists or performers, who also travel widely and who personify the vitality of the cultures which they perpetuate. But they demonstrate individual uniqueness as well, and it is safer for a state or society to lay claim to universally great works created or collected by ancestors long before any contemporary political issue came into being.

In the examples discussed here, exhibitions of works owned or created by the sponsor's society have traveled to various American museums, often through mediation of the U.S. State Department. The exhibitions have varied in the aesthetic qualities of the artworks themselves, the publicity or other interpretation put upon them, the size and social location of the audience to be attracted and persuaded and, foremost and determining of these other variables, the nature of the political agenda of both sponsor and host. Depending upon this latter variable, the former ones link together in exhibitions to be disinterestedly understood as art, or self-interestedly arranged for the propagandistic purposes of the museums themselves or of the competing states.

Either way, the artworks selected must be of superior aesthetic quality if they are to be accepted by the elites who interpret the works for the wider, less sophisticated audience. Reviewers have varied in their willingness to take sides in the diplomatic agendas, by either ignoring or loudly proclaiming the nonaesthetic purposes of sponsors of museum blockbusters. Yet the more important the political agendas and propaganda become, the more overwhelming and aesthetically powerful must be the works which carry them symbolically, and the more readily are art critics "co-opted" into discussing only the art. Of course, in addition to artistic interpretations of politically-freighted blockbuster exhibitions, press coverage is usually given to their economic impacts. Since this is usually assessed in terms of profits to the host city and institution, the exhibition sponsor is interpreted as benefiting the audiences not just spiritually, by allowing them access to this great art, but economically as well. The sponsor is thus presented as a participant in a free market of the world economic order and in the free market of culture and artistic creativity, as conservator of the world's patrimony on all counts.

While many have decried the increasing political manipulation of artworks by states for propagandistic purposes, their commercial manipulation is less commonly criticized, at least by those who favor the ostensibly free market of capitalism. From the left, a critique such as Walter Benjamin's (1960) makes sense: the unique qualities of individual artworks, experienced "face-to-face," are indeed cheapened as they are made commonly available through the kind of mechanical reproduction that accompanies blockbuster exhibitions. But Edward Banfield's (1984) argument that any form of government subsidy is inherently corruptive of aesthetic experience would seem no more persuasive than Benjamin's case against commercialization. Neither position recognizes that artworks are inevitably preserved and displayed for less-than-purely aesthetic reasons. Indeed, it is the elective affinity between great artworks and those who possess great political, economic or religious power that makes them so symbolically meaningful to the multitudes who must encounter them if any claim to "universal" significance is to be plausible. If great art is to sacralize secular pursuits, the halo effect either works reflectively in the other direction as well, or it does not work at all.

In any event, the alternative of "art-for-art's sake"—as so often proclaimed by the artworlds and particularly the museums involved in international exchanges such as described here—is recognized by all concerned to have both political and economic consequences. Indeed, such recognition contributes much to its appeal as a rationale for state support for the arts, in any fashion.

Thus those with political or economic agendas, as well as those whose purposes are primarily aesthetic, are increasingly caught in a dilemma of their own cooperative making. In many ways, all have mutually benefited from their symbiotic relationships, and the increased rationalization of the processes by which these are effected. Institutional and legal mechanisms are in place to facilitate the use of artworks as cultural ambassadors, whenever international politics, economics, or even religion finds it advantageous. But once the "friendly" competition of symbol systems is enjoined internationally through the use of the arts, one cannot opt out of the game. Even allied states must maintain visibility in each others' museums and galleries, concert halls and theaters, to increasingly sophisticated audiences who now expect varieties of propagandistic "halos" around visiting artworks, and take that expectation into account. All the more must the installation and interpretation of major loan exhibitions be carefully orchestrated by sponsors and hosts, and all the more is such show-biz seen for what it is.

Over all, however, it is clear that of all the variables considered in this comparison of museum blockbusters, the irreducible factor is the aesthetic power of the artworks so obligingly co-opted for other purposes. Such propagandistic uses are effective only if the art remains, in some measure through its own qualities, transcendent. As such, in a general sense, the universal and individualizing values expressed in great art stand as judge and measure of those who would use it for their own purposes. The same elusive qualities which make the arts so difficult to analyze sociologically or to use for propaganda purposes may ultimately contribute most to their survival.

## Notes

1. Unlike Nelson Rockefeller's promotion of the arts in international exchanges out of his own deep appreciation of them, Nixon apparently so involved himself for purely political reasons. On the domestic front he was more than antipathetic toward the artworld institutions in which such exchanges are enshrined: just before his resignation it was made known that during the 1972 election campaign he had kept his staff, and especially his daughter, away from any events held at museums, as these were invariably filled with "Jews and left-wing types" (*The New York Times,* Aug. 7, 1974).
2. Hammer subsequently pleaded guilty in federal court to charges of making illegal contributions to the 1972 Nixon campaign.
3. The complicated history of the show "Treasures of the Holy Land: Ancient Art from the Israel Museum" chronicles as well the changing patterns of American-Israeli-Arab relations since the exhibition was first proposed in 1982. Some of the objects to be included came from a museum in East Jerusalem, taken by the Israelis in the "Six-Day War" of 1967, and therefore still claimed by Arabs. Since their ownership was in dispute, the original American host museums (the Metropolitan and the Smithsonian) cancelled the show as a security risk, presumably due to the absence of State Department approval necessary for insurance coverage. By 1985, despite (or perhaps because) of anti-Israeli terrorist attacks, that approval was forthcoming, and the show was rescheduled—still including objects from disputed territory. However, any political overtones due to "blockbuster hype" were disclaimed. According to a Met Museum spokesman, "It won't be everyone's cup of tea . . .It's the kind of show where the viewer will have to do some work, not like, say, a Rubens show where the color helps to seduce you" (*The New York Times,* Jan. 1, 1986).

## References

Balfe, J. H. (1985a). "Introduction," *Art, Ideology, & Politics.* Judith H. Balfe & Margaret Wyszomirski (eds.) N. Y.: Praeger.

(1985b). "Art Style as Political Actor: Social Realism and Its Alternatives." *Sociologia Internationalis* 23:1. 3–26.

Banfield, E. (1984). *The Democratic Muse.* N. Y.: Basic Books.

Benjamin, W. (1960). "Works of Art in the Age of Mechanical Reproduction." *Studies on the Left* I. 28–40.

Bensman, J., & Vidich, A. (1971). *The New American Society.* Chicago: Quadrangle Books.

Bower, R. T., & Sharp, L. M. (1956). "The Use of Art in International Communication: a Case Study." *Public Opinion Quarterly* 20:1. 221–229.

Cockcroft, E. (1974). "Abstract Expressionism: Weapon of the Cold War." *Artforum* 12. 39–41.

Goodman, W. (1977). "The Artist and the Politician: Natural Antagonists?" *The New York Times,* April 24. Section 2:1.

Guerman, M. (1979). *The Art of the October Revolution.* N. Y.: Harry Abrams.

Guilbault, S. (1984). *How New York Stole the Idea of Modern Art.* Chicago: University of Chicago Press.

Hall, S. S. (1983). "The Art of the Popes Comes to America." *The New York Times Magazine,* Jan. 16. 12 ff.

Kramer, H. (1975). "Reconsiderations on the Art of Détente." *The New York Times,* Oct. 30. 50.

(1977). "Détente Yields a Dismal Show." *The New York Times,* April 24. D25.

(1980). "Bronze Age Chinese Art Starts U.S. Tour at the Met." *The New York Times,* April 11. C1.

(1982). "A Note on The New Criterion." *The New Criterion* I:1. 1–5.

Larson, G. O. (1983). *The Reluctant Patron*. Philadelphia: University of Pennsylvania Press.
Lerman, L. (1970). *The Museum: 100 Years and the Metropolitan Museum*. N. Y.: Viking.
Meyer, K. (1979). *The Art Museum: Power, Money, Ethics*. N. Y.: William Morrow.
Moiseyev, I. (1984). "Cultural Exchange: One Way to Learn." *The New York Times*, Feb. 18. 35.
*The New York Times* (1973). "Chinese Art Treasures Thrill Paris." May 9. 40.
(1973). "Pope Opens Vatican Gallery of Modern Art Holding 600 Works." June 24. 3.
(1973). "Chinese Art Show Coming to Capital." Oct. 30. 40.
(1974). "An Impressive but 'Propagandistic' Show of Chinese Art." Aug. 25. II:1.
(1974). "Art Officials Deplore Nixon Comment." Aug. 7. 22.
(1976). "Are Art Exchanges a Game of Propaganda?" quoting Peter Solmssen. Sept. 26. B:1.
(1977). "Art People," quoting Leo Castelli. Jan. 21. C18.
(1977). "Art v. Politics and the Venice Biennale." Nov. 10. 29.
(1977). "Show of U.S. Paintings Opens in Moscow." Dec. 22. C18.
(1979). "The 'Crown Jewels' from the Kremlin." May 13. II:1.
(1980). "Plan to Put Soviet Art Show in Armory Stirs Dispute." Jan. 10. 53.
(1980). "Veterans Win Armory Battle." Jan. 11. 36.
(1982). "Jewish Groups Protest Met's Decision Against Israel Show." quoting Morris Abram. Feb. 25. B57.
(1982). "Kollek Attacks Met on Israeli Show." quoting Teddy Kollek. Feb. 27. 11.
(1983). "Vatican Show Visitors Spend $101 Million in City." Aug. 22. B63.
(1984). "Soviet Musicians Perform at Museum." April 4. B37.
(1985). "U.S.-Soviet Art Exchange Planned." Dec. 14. 15.
(1986). "200 Objects Picked for Disputed Israel Show at Met." Jan. 1. 9.
Russell, J. (1974). "Beauty Fills the Chinese Exhibit in Toronto." *The New York Times*. Aug. 9. 35.
Simon, N. (1972). "Simon Says 'Under One Roof We'd Rank among the Top Museums in the Country'." *ARTnews*. Dec. 2. 24.

# Nature as News: Science Reporting in *The New York Times* 1898 to 1983

Charles R. Simpson

Commercial newspapers not overtly tied to political parties or sponsored by governments can be understood to contain two types of news: stories about society and stories about nature. The first category, "social stories," includes coverage of the humanly constructed environment: politics, crime, the marketplace. Typical "social stories" convey a critical or evaluative response to the happenings they report. Individual stories comprise parts of a broader mosaic of social history in which the interpretation of daily events in the newspaper merges with and reinforces the elements of the reader's direct experience. The two forms of experience, first-hand and newspaper-mediated, interact in memory to form a composite. Because the newspaper comprises hardcopy which is retrievable and because its message is widely distributed, it gains authority as an intersubjective anchorage for personal recollection. The microfilming of "newspapers of record" such as *The New York Times* has advanced this process of focusing individual memory of collective events around newspaper copy. Through newspapers, and especially their "social stories," the individual locates him or herself within an historical topography. Daily life, at least in retrospect, can take on an epic dimension.

The second category of newspaper article is "nature stories." These discuss the relationship of mankind to the natural environment: storms, disease, drought and the intellectual challenge posed by nature. "Nature stories" and "social stories" can be considered two conceptual systems within the same text, the newspaper. According to the Swiss linguist Ferdinand de Saussure, we can expect that conceptual subsystems will be defined

* Presented at the Social Theory, Politics and the Arts Conference. The New School for Social Research, New York City, October 25–27, 1985.
The author wishes to thank Susan Sweeney-Patnode for her research assistance; and Arthur J. Vidich and Michael W. Hughley for editorial suggestions.

28 [218]

in opposition to one another. "Concepts are purely differential and defined not by their positive content but negatively by their relations with the other terms of the system."[1] The meaning of concepts in a text, then, lies in "being what the others are not."[2] This paper suggests that stories about the natural environment and the social environment should be understood to be in tension with one another, and that reports about science and nature in the newspaper qualify the meaning of political and economic news.

Alfred Schutz has written that "the meaning of the elements of the social world in all its diversity and stratification, as well as the pattern of its texture itself, is by those living within it just taken for granted."[3] This paper suggests that elements of the social world as reported in the newspaper differ in their taken-for-granted character. In particular societies at particular times, reports which mediate between individuals and the social world and interpret that world are likely to be met with considerable skepticism. However, reports about the natural environment are less obtrusively ideological or biased than political and economic news. Stories about weather or disease do not seem to be vehicles suited for carrying biases. If political and philosophical assumptions are contained in news about the natural environment, they are more apt to have Schutz's "taken-for-granted" quality. Their apparent objectivity can be important in transmitting ideology to readers.

News about nature conveys the contours of collective social experience. Utilizing Karl Mannheim's typology of the variety of historico-philosophical perspectives available to social classes in the modern world, we can expect that newspapers express differing perspectives on historical change. This study finds that *The New York Times* expresses the liberal view.[4] Liberals, like Chiliasts, contrast the present state of the human condition with ideals attainable only in the future. But unlike Chiliasts, liberals see a line of continuity and remediation connecting present problems with an ideal future. Hope for progress, then, lies with change which is incremental rather than catastrophic. Because its understanding of history embodies progress, liberalism appeals to that class which sees its interests advancing within existing organizational structures of society. The attitude toward social problems and the future is optimistic.

> The normative-liberal mentality also (like the Chiliast) contains this qualitative differentiation of historical events, and in addition holds in contempt as an evil reality everything that has become a part

of the past or is a part of the present. It defers the actual realization
of these norms into the remote future and, at the same time, unlike
the Chiliast who anticipates its realization at some ecstatic point
beyond history, it sees it as arising out of the process of becoming
in the here and now, out of the process of everyday life. From this
has developed, we have seen, the typically linear conception of
evolution and the relatively direct connection between a formerly
transcendental and meaningful goal and present actual experience.[5]

Social stories and nature stories together help liberal newspapers
convey a linear and progressive view of the historical process as
objectively descriptive. This paper analyzes the ways in which news
of the natural environment contributes to the liberal historico-
political perspective embodied in *The Times* over the last century.

## Methodology

Data for this study was obtained from two sources. First, studies
of *The New York Times* by employees and journalists have been
examined for information on articles and editorial policy concerned
with news of the natural environment. Information obtained from
these accounts is, however, anecdotal. While existing studies of
*The Times* are chronological, they have not focused on science
reporting or systematically looked at its development as a news
specialization.

The second source of information about nature news in *The Times*
was obtained by making a survey and analysis of the content of
articles on hazards and the natural environment which appeared
in the paper between 1898 and 1983. *The Times* was surveyed at
five year intervals. In each survey year one day's issue was
analyzed each month. Days were selected following the order of
the week. This method was used to eliminate bias introduced by
linkage of science news with a particular day of the week and
to compensate for the larger Sunday issue. In the first portion of
the analysis, format standardization of weather reporting was
studied. Next, a total of 355 articles about nature as a hazardous
environment were identified. These were recorded by year of
appearance and coded by dominant content type: nature as routine
and predictable, the character and direction of scientific inquiry,
and the relationship between catastrophe and community. The
conceptual focuses utilized in each category and its subcategories

will be discussed in the analysis. A longitudinal study was used to reveal any shifts over time in the thematic treatment of this type of science news. Such shifts have taken place. They correlate with large themes in political and economic news: World Wars I and II, the period of aviation development and the exploration of remote places in the 1920s and again in the 1970s, the Great Depression, and the post-war period of nuclear rivalry between the superpowers.

## The Routinization of the Natural World

The most frequent treatment of the natural environment in *The New York Times* in the 20th century is as a routine event. Each issue of the paper carries a local weather forecast in the upper right corner of the front page. This balances the paper's slogan, "All the News That's Fit to Print," contained in a box in the upper left of that page. The symmetry is not without significance. The objectivity and impartiality presumed in the precis of the coming weather supports parallel claims to accuracy and completeness in social news.

Extended but still routine coverage of weather occurs in the body of the paper. In 1898 approximately five percent of a page was devoted to standardized weather coverage while by 1983 half a page was utilized. While there is a practical value to forecasting the day's temperatures and precipitation, even for a nonfarm readership, the amount of detail provided is far in excess of what the New York resident needs to know in order to dress appropriately.

*The Times* began reporting local weather conditions and making daily forecasts in the 1850s, and by 1898 these reports had accumulated a baroque embellishment. In that year articles on the weather contained the following information: national patterns of barometric pressure, temperature and storm activity; a record of the temperature in the city for the last 24 hours, taken at two to four hour intervals from two locations and contrasted with the city's readings of the previous year; the previous day's maximum and minimum temperatures and the time these occurred along with humidity recorded at two points in time. *The Times* relied on data from the National Weather Bureau for most of its information, but added readings from its own thermometer "six feet above the street level" in Printing House Square. In its regularity and complexity, weather reporting was already a ritual by 1898. The convolutions of its detail followed not practical need but an imperative of objectivity raised to an aesthetic.

Coverage of the weather in normal circumstances has become a newspaper ritual, important for its regularity and aura of statistical exactitude. As early as 1898 it conveyed an image of *The Times* as comprehensive and objective, envisioning the entire continent and reporting singular events in precise terms to an audience without apparent class differentiation.

Over time, a growing number of weather stations in the United States and abroad were added to the National Weather Bureau's network and *The Times* was able to expand its coverage. To a degree, this increased coverage of ordinary weather had a practical basis. Modes of transportation were changing and air travel in particular gave New Yorkers an interest in the specifics of weather over wider regions. By 1928 the paper was devoting five column inches to a "Forecast of Flying Weather," derived from the National Weather Bureau. The weather in major European cities and 44 American cities was capsuled. As a service to speculators in the commodity exchanges, *The Times* gave accounts of the weather in each of the cotton and grain-producing states. The possibility that some might profit from hail or drought that ruined others, however, was an implicitly jarring departure from the classless aspect of weather. It was dropped by the 1950s.

The tradition of special-service weather bulletins has continued, though without invidious overtones. It presently extends to a summer recreational forecast which gives tide times, temperatures and precipitation at beaches and mountains, and gardening-related information.[6] However much weather reporting is an occasion for newspapers to appear objective and in the public interest, it is hung on a peg of practicality. Since the National Weather Bureau supplies this information in a readily publishable form, it is not surprising that newspapers take the weather seriously and support the government's role in the collection of requisite data.[7]

By the 1950s weather reporting was more comprehensive and technical than ever. National maps of wind, temperature and atmospheric pressure were featured. Local temperature and humidity readings were given on an hourly basis for the previous day and apparent movements of the sun and moon were recorded. Flying forecasts were dropped, but temperatures in additional cities abroad were reported. The 1978 issues of *The Times* included satellite photographs of the continent showing large weather patterns. These photos, obtained from the National Oceanic and Atmospheric Administration, provide an impressive visual symbol of newspaper omniscience and objectivity. They enabled *The Times*, in god-like fashion, to behold the entire globe.

Feature articles on the routine character of a variety of natural events have appeared in 18 of the 20 years surveyed. In these, the regularity, predictability and increasing comprehensibility of natural events is the dominant theme.

There were three periods when such articles were most frequent: 1898, 1933 to 1938, and 1983. In the 1898 period, *The Times* was able to report on the expansion of the weather data network into such areas as Haiti, and stories on the routinization of natural events reached 25% of all articles on nature. During the two Depression years surveyed, stories stressing the growing intelligibility of nature comprised 23% of all stories on the natural environment. In a decade of dustbowls, grasshopper plagues and farm foreclosures, *The Times* interspersed reassuring images of the natural world. In 1933 it ran a story on page one titled "Weather to be Same 23 Years From Now," which said that a "fundamental climatological interval, second only to the year itself," had been found.[8] In 1938, the paper reported on page one that Soviet explorers aboard an icebreaker 300 miles from the North Pole had concluded that the Arctic region and the entire world was growing warmer.[9] *The Times* was informing its readers that the character of the natural environment was neither chaotic nor ultimately hostile to mankind. The sometimes catastrophic peculiarities of climate were now intelligible. Thirty years later, in 1968, *The Times* reported that according to American scientists "extensive weather modification might be possible within two decades."[10] International cooperation was called for. Somewhat closer to the ground, of course, the war in Vietnam was reaching a peak of intensity and controversy.

In 1983 articles on the routinization of natural events comprised 28.6% of all stories on nature. In 1978 *The Times* introduced a weekly section on science as part of a major redesign of the paper. This section was published every Tuesday, and greatly increased the coverage of science related news.

When natural catastrophe strikes, a subform of routinization occurs in *The Times*, an after-the-fact survey of similar events down through the years. These surveys facilitate the reader's adjustment to a specific disaster by locating it within the broader historical continuum of events. However great the death toll, the associated type of human activity—fishing, ocean transport—is shown to continue. A chronology allows the reader to measure the present event by an historical yardstick. This contextualization lets readers discuss the tragedy in comparative terms.[11]

Disaster chronologies are collective obituaries of the dead. Public acknowledgement of individual death and an orderly accounting of the losses helps to heal the pain and place it in perspective. This is the function of memorialization.[12] The living affirm their difference from as well as communal solidarity with the deceased. Collective society, integrated by grief or at least remembrance, continues. In these instances, articles on the natural environment affirm the moral coherence and continuity of the social world. Having expanded the readers' awareness of catastrophic events beyond the local scene and so adding a burden of diffuse grief, the newspaper then provides funeral rites to discharge that grief. In this sense the newspaper organizes and orchestrates the collective rituals of loss, grief and remembrance for a modern mass society in which peoples' career paths are tied to organizations rather than to localities. Whereas funeral rites affirming the solidarity of the living through their reverence for the dead were face-to-face in primitive societies, such ceremonies are newspaper-mediated in mass society. Instruments of mass communication maintain at least a semblance of emotional integration in the national community.

## The March of Science

In 15 of the 18 years sampled, *The New York Times* carried stories which emphasized the character and direction of science and technology in history. Three historical directions or paradigms for the conceptualization of science emerged: science was progressively enhancing the human condition and subjugating nature; human knowledge was destroying the natural world and, ultimately, human life chances; and while the control of nature in some areas might be possible, there were limits to what mankind could or should do in pacifying the natural environment.

In 13 of these years, science was depicted as in the process of defeating the ancient enemies of civilization, especially disease. One such story occurred in 1908 and is characteristic of the newspaper's emphasis on the vigilance required to secure the advance of society over nature. The story is titled "How Plagues are Watched the World Around," and in a map and a half page of text describes how Alvah H. Doty, Health Officer of the Port of New York, is able to utilize "a unique system of espionage" in order to "guard against the entrance into this country of death-dealing diseases."[13] Cases of bubonic plague, cholera and yellow fever are mapped by Officer Doty as they occur around the world. He then inspects vessels entering the city's harbor, giving particular attention to those which have landed at ports reporting disease. A world system of medical cooperation makes this surveillance possible, with useful help from the Germans and the Japanese. But threats continuously exist from less enlightened parts of the globe, particularly Russia, China and India. *The Times* identifies the problem as one of religious underdevelopment:

> The pilgrimages to Mecca, the 'exalted' holy of holies of the Mohammedans, are the one great cause and the statistics prove it. The Mohammedans, as all the world knows, make these pilgrimages to 'The Mother of Cities' in great unclean hordes sleeping on decks of dirty ships, drinking water that has never been pure, and eating food in which the germ of cholera and the plague are sometimes known to exist. These ships touch at ports, and the pilgrims come in contact with people of other countries. The result is the spread of cholera and plague.[14]

Advanced societies must utilize their technology to insure that they do not import the failures of lagging regions. News of science reinforced the social-Darwinist assumptions of the time.

The protection of Americans against disease originating in foreign lands was complicated by World War I when United States citizens were overseas in large numbers. The government was shown to be equal to the task, however. In March 1918, for example, *The Times* reported that 60 enlisted men in the U.S. Sanitary Corps., all from New England, were being exposed to lice known to carry trench fever.[15] So far, however, the "organism producing the fever" had eluded the microscope. Later that same year the Health Commissioner of New York was reported to have announced that his department had discovered a vaccine to prevent Spanish influenza.[16] Influenza, a greater killer than enemy troops during 1914–18 war, was not stopped, however. It remained an object of scientific effort for the rest of the century, periodic victory announcements notwithstanding.

Only one article on the fight against disease was coded during the two Depression years surveyed. This emphasized public health measures. It praised the efforts of the Tennessee Valley Authority for designing lakes and reservoirs to eliminate the breeding areas of malaria-carrying mosquitoes.[17] The responsibility for the eradication of disease legitimated an expanded role for the state from 1908 on.

In the World War II period, articles on advances in the scientific control of nature had to find a place within a newspaper restructured to meet the national emergency. Newsprint was not readily available, and while *The Times* had its own source, a wholly-owned plant in Canada, it complied with paper rationing. In addition, the newspaper's effort to comprehensively report a global conflict meant that war news encroached on all other departments. Advertising often could not be printed due to lack of space.[18]

As the scientific establishment was mobilized into the war effort, reports on science came to include the relevance of particular discoveries to victory over the Axis. In 1943 the newspaper carried a story from *Science* magazine on the first successful synthesis of biotin, the 'life' vitamin.[19] The article expressed the hope that this 'super vitamin,' essential to all life functions, would aid in protecting Allied troops now afflicted with malaria.

Disease, particularly in the case of Allied troops, was discussed as an externally caused affliction, not the fault of scientists, government officials or victims. In June of 1943, *The Times* announced that the Army had found the incidence of venereal disease among American troops in England to be 25 times higher than at home.[20] Human fault existed, but where? The attractiveness and aggressive salesmanship of London's prostitutes was found to be the cause. The cure lay in the Army's program of opening up prophylactic stations in Red Cross clubs.

The march of science continued in the post-war period. Cholera found in Rome and other Italian cities in 1973 was "no cause for alarm" because government programs of vaccination were thorough.[21] In 1978 scientists were reported to have found the virus that was thought to cause hepatitis.[22] When disastrous floods in Southeast Asia caused Vietnam to ask for food relief for 2.7 million people, the newspaper reported that "a knowledgeable international official" believed modern pesticides, spraying equipment and new strains of rice, particularly IR-36 developed at the Rice Institute in the Philippines, were required to eliminate Vietnam's deep-seated food production problems.[23] That country's immediately prior experience with herbicidal defoliation of forests and rice acreage during the war was not mentioned.

Throughout the period surveyed, *The Times* published articles which described problems of disease and famine as being steadily overcome by advances in science and technology. The United States and the industrially developed world were consequently becoming safer places. Nature was being progressively subordinated to mankind. Governments, particularly America's, were the most important agents in this struggle and were to that extent legitimated.

*Surrogate Survival*

A subcategory of the march of science deals with exploration on the edges of the known world. The poles, jungles, deserts and eventually outer space were locales for tales which combined adventure with a scientific purpose. These stories included personal confrontation with hardship and danger. Systematic preparation, courage and undeniable luck enabled the scientific adventurers to reach and reveal their unknown worlds. Both these worlds and the struggle to reach them were news.

The first *Times* exploration story occurred in 1886, and publicized a Lieutenant Schwatka's trip to the west coast of Alaska. After World War I, the number of these stories increased. According to *Times* historian and reporter Meyer Berger, from 1923 to 1949 there was barely a season without "some first-hand account of man's thrilling air, sea and land conquests; of expeditions to Tibet, to the lost Incan and Mayan cities, to the jungles of Africa, South America, Asia and Central America."[24] During the Depression, *Times* publisher Adolph Ochs intentionally used these stories to "counterbalance the dark side of the news."[25] *The Times* might be said to have invented Indiana Jones, the archeologist-adventurer of film and novelization. This fictional character represents a liberal image in popular culture of the activist intellectual and has equated university fieldwork with the fedora.

A high point was the securing of exclusive New York rights to publish the story of the discovery of the tomb of Tutankhamen in the Egyptian desert. When a reporter for *The Times* of London entered the tomb on December 21, 1922 and described "what it looked like after 30 centuries as a royal dwelling place," *New York Times* editor Carl Van Anda ran it on page one.[26]

Another of these articles dealt with Roald Amundsen's 55-day exploration of the Antarctic in 1912, and was described as "a thrilling story."[27] *The Times* purchased the exclusive rights to publish Amundsen's tale and delayed announcement of his successful arrival at the South Pole until they were ready to print the full story.

Subsequent expeditions were similarly underwritten by the newspaper. When they became available, radio transmitters were provided to explorers and *The Times* was able to quickly report their progress. Admiral Richard E. Byrd's flight over the South Pole in 1926 was so sponsored and equipped. It resulted in a ten day series in *The Times* by Byrd himself and the naming of bits of the landscape after members of the publisher's family.[28]

The activist-intellectual image has suited the paper's own reporters. They venerated Billy Kennedy who, by courage and deception, secured an exclusive story of a ship loss and ocean rescue in 1886. Injured in a free-for-all with the rescue ship's crew and forced to dive over the rail into pitch blackness, Kennedy survived and spent the trip back to New York editing his copy with bandaged hands.[29] War correspondents wrote in this tradition. Their exploits, including capture by the enemy and in two instances death on the front lines, became part of the tradition of reporting at *The Times*.[30] In the postwar period, Harrison Salisbury's reports from Hanoi on the secret American bombing of North Vietnam in 1966 and Herbert Matthews' exclusive interviews with Fidel Castro at his mountain retreat in 1957 sustained the adventurer-reporter ideal.[31] It is not surprising that reporters and editors looked for scientific stories which had similar components of engagement and heroism.

### Man As The Enemy of Nature

Stories in this category focus on the destruction of nature and natural processes by human action, resulting in a consequent threat to the social environment. While such stories exist in *The Times*, this survey indicates that they are rare. Only one was found in the systematic survey, a poisoning of Lake Champlain by a lumber mill.

### Science and the Recognition of Human Limits

In the last half of the century, a new element appeared in *The Times* editorials and news reports. For the first time, doubt was

Simpson, Charles R.                    [229] 39

cast on the ability of scientists and engineers to conquer nature
in a definitive way. In these stories, the boundary between the
humanly contrived world and that dominated by nature was not
definitively secured. Advances in medicine were seen as subject
to circumvention by natural processes. Rather than being a
landscape yielding to heroic exploration, nature was conceded to
be an active force capable of neutralizing human effort. Some
scientific gains were merely provisional.

This new conceptualization of nature was introduced selectively
with the European floods and Southwestern United States droughts
of 1953. From that time on it has co-existed with the older
perspective which celebrates technological progress against nature
as Promethean.

Three rationales for a more guarded assessment of the
relationship of mankind to nature can be detected. First, nature
continued to generate events which resulted in sweeping
devastation. But air surveillance and transportation technology,
greatly improved during World War II, allowed reporters to witness
and describe remote catastrophes. Journalists could now fly over
miles of flooded countryside and had access to more reliable
government statistics on deaths and property damage. It became
more difficult to contextualize disasters as exceptional events which
communities could repair.

Second, scientific research in bacteria and viruses revealed that
nature, far from presenting mankind with a fixed set of puzzles,
was a creative antagonist. It circumvented immune systems and
outmaneuvered pharmacological weapons. The suspicion grew that
permanent victory over many diseases was not possible.

Third, *The Times* began to recognize that the modernization of
society had diminished the margin of safety previously available
to mitigate human mistakes. Technology had risks. Changes in
farm practices—monoculture over large areas using an array of
chemical sprays—now revealed a latent aspect. Infestation became
more resistant and groundwater supplies were contaminated.
Metropolitan growth resulted in greater reliance on water systems,
transportation networks and communication. Once disruptions
occurred they often became calamities. Warfare appeared less an
instrument of national defense than a route to human extinction.

By 1958 *The Times* reported that recipients of polio vaccine who
contracted the disease from innoculations were winning lawsuits
against drug manufacturers; Dr. Jonas Salk, the vaccine's
discoverer and hero to parents, was on the witness stand for the

defense.[32] In 1963 the newspaper reported that "U.S. Scientists Doubt Worth of Flu Shots." Despite 42 million immunization shots, 1,000 Americans a week were dying of influenza and pneumonia.[33] The Army Corps of Engineers gave up trying to safeguard residents of Montz, Louisiana from periodic floods and ordered them evacuated and their houses destroyed.[34] In 1983 bubonic plague surfaced as a modern problem in New Mexico; the chaos of the middle ages seemed to hover behind the apparent order of the modern world. As individuals took sick and died, residents conducted a ritual slaughter of prairie dogs.[35]

Without abandoning the celebration of mankind's mastery over nature—the march of science motif—*The Times* developed a countertheme in the 1950s and has continued it into the present. Increasingly, articles suggested that mankind learn to accept that some things could not be done and others were better left undone. These recent doubts raised about the progressive direction of science suggest that liberalism as an historical perspective, and with it the self-confidence of a class, was weakening.

### Catastrophe and the Construction of Moral Community

Of the 355 stories identified, the largest category of article was that which dealt with impending or actual disruption of community life by natural forces. Localities were frequently badly damaged in these stories, but the social entity of community was not destroyed. Stories of natural disaster affirmed the reality of a community of values, interdependence and mutual aid for a mass society in which the emotional solidarity of local community had become a nostalgic impulse.

Catastrophes were utilized to spotlight the recuperative strengths of communities: the heroism of neighbors, the dedication of health personnel, the willingness of government to rush outside aid to those whose best efforts merited the help of the wider society. The fact/that natural disaster was site-specific and apparently random allowed *The Times* to focus its attention on localities which ordinarily would not generate news and whose heroism or grim stoicism could be inferred to be characteristic of any community in the United States. The moral qualities of foreign localities were somewhat less certain. An alternative hypothesis, that moral community was largely a temporary response to locality-wide disaster, neither characteristic of all settlements nor enduring, was never considered.

America's hamlets and cities worked as moral as well as functional environments, *The Times* said. They even worked in the midst of disaster. When life was disrupted, neighbors, rescue squad members, government officials and, on occasion, the business sector worked efficiently to return communities to normal functioning. This coverage of a tornado in Gainsville was typical.

> The physicians who have assisted in the work of relief say that the scenes at the mills were appalling, the victims being crushed and mangled in every conceivable manner. . . . As soon as the tornado had passed those who were not disabled immediately went to work rescuing the victims. All the stores in the business section that were not hit closed their doors, and every male citizen who could lend a hand promptly joined in the work of rescue. . . .
>
> The local physicians were unable to cope with the situation and surgeons and medical supplies have been ordered sent from Atlanta. A special train carrying a corps of surgeons and supplies arrived to-night, making the total number of physicians now in the city about forty.[36]

Throughout the century, it was clear in these stories that modernization had not eroded the selfless concern of neighbors for one another. These articles on natural disaster are broadly ideological. They affirm to the readership the reality of moral community, usually somewhere else, which has survived the marketplace. By implication, all localities remain morally integrated communities, awaiting only a disaster to make this more visible.

The newspaper vicariously involves its readers in the moral community about which it reports. Since these reports are standardized over time, they take on a ritual quality which celebrates and reinforces the moral values by which individuals meet disaster. *The Times* gives public recognition and sanction to values which may exist only as a response to disaster and are not operative in the ordinary world. In this sense, *The Times* sustains an image of collective life—one based on small town virtues of neighborliness, helpfulness and civic mindedness— which is certainly not the daily world of its primary readers in New York City. Thus *The Times* involves even blasé and socially suspicious urbanites in a ritually sustained image of community virtues which is emotionally rewarding.

The items in the category of catastrophe and community were coded for content prior to being broken down into subcategories. The setting for 44% was urban, but a surprisingly large 36% were rural, with 20% taking place on the water. Cities were safer refuges from nature than the surrounding sea and countryside. Not surprisingly, stories on American localities dominated catastrophe reporting in *The Times*. Sixty-four percent of disaster stories dealt with the United States and the Atlantic Ocean, with an additional 11% on the rest of North America. Seven percent dealt with Europe, with the rest scattered throughout the globe. Only three percent dealt with South and Central America. In disaster visibility, nearness and social similarity count.

Thirty percent of natural disasters reported were windstorms: hurricanes, tornadoes, gales. Windstorms are particularly suited for dramatic narration. They move and can be discussed as impending events as well as realized catastrophes. Epidemic disease, sharing the quality of locomotion, accounted for 13% of the cases. Floods, both inland and coastal, were the subject of 16% of the stories. They too had a history, waxing and waning, and generated suspense. Earthquakes comprised 11% of reported events, the same as blizzards and severe cold or snowfall. An assortment of insect damage, animal damage, drought and heat comprised the remainder. The journalistic aesthetic favors natural catastrophes which involve proximity, suspense, a stunning degree of destruction, and heroic recovery.

One man with a child in his arms, holding the little child above his shoulders, started to cross the dams with the water up to his body. His wife, with another child, stood in the window of their house, the floor of which was already flooded by the rising water, and watched her husband feel his way step by step along the top of the treacherous dam, one false step from which or a caving bank would throw him into a swift moving current. Finally he was sighted from across the river on the city side. A boat was put off, and after half an hour's effort the family was rescued.[37]

While stories contained discussion of several types of damage, the reported effects of catastrophes included death or illness in 51% of the cases. Homelessness was a factor in 32% of the stories, with forced relocation occurring in 11% of cases. Fear, depression or anxiety were mentioned in 27% of the stories.

It might be expected that human failing would be a contributing cause in natural disasters. Readers of *The Times*, however, did not often learn this. In less than seven percent of cases was human responsibility a contributing factor in a natural catastrophe. When humans were negligent, the fault lay equally with officials, the private economic sector, and human nature. Foolish or knavish officials were usually in foreign governments. Their lapses were attributed to greed, and took the form of poor planning or poor execution of relief measures.[38]

When the private sector failed in its responsibilities, it was due to avoidable ignorance in planning for or responding to disaster. Two-thirds of these cases were European, one-third American. Victims, too, might conceivably share blame in the events surrounding a natural disaster. This occurred only two percent of the time, and was attributed to ignorance. Thus, a Mexican epidemic of yellow fever in 1903 is blamed on "the failure of the lower class of Mexicans to report cases of the disease to the health authorities."[39] In America, at least, disaster was not a time for recriminations which would divide communities and impede the cooperation necessary for recovery, according to *The Times*.

The image of localities as morally and functionally integrated communities included a lack of attention to the class-characteristics of victims. Like rain from heaven, natural disaster seemed to fall on all and level differences in station. In 61% of cases, class could not be determined from the stories. In five percent of cases, victims were conspicuously poor, and in five percent middle class. Where individuals were occupationally designated, their class was clear but they were usually depicted as comprising communities unto themselves rather than segments of more heterogeneous localities. In 29% of cases victims were working class—sailors, miners, agricultural workers, small farmers. It is characteristic of the ritually integrative function of *The Times* disaster reporting to transcend community divisions.

Catastrophe frequently brought out latent heroism in ordinary individuals. Victims in 11% of reported events heroically sought to save others and in two percent of cases demonstrated notable determination to save themselves. In heroism lies much of the narrative drama of disaster stories in *The Times*.

Mrs. George Marcotte and six of her children were among the drowning victims in Portneuf. Four of the bodies were recovered late this afternoon. At dawn, Mrs. Marcotte was awakened by the sound of water beating against the foundations of their wooden home. Guiding her eleven children out of the building, with anything they could grab in the way of clothing, the family started toward higher ground. Five of them succeeded in making their escape, but the others, forced to clutch trees for safety, slipped from them one by one as their hands chilled, and dropped to their deaths as their home swirled by in the grip of the current.[40]

Tragedy can be redeemed in part by miracles. In the same Quebec floods described above, another victim was Mrs. Corinthin Audet, mother of a one-day-old child: "The infant was in her arms, crying, when the mother's body was taken from the ruins."[41]

In 35% of cases, victims acted responsibly but not specifically with heroism. In the remainder of cases their behavior could not be determined. Rescuers on the scene were specifically described as responsive to the need of others 25% of the time; in an additional 11% of cases they were fully heroic. In no article were rescuers craven. Relentless effort and a willingness to assume personal risk characterized rescuers.[42] In only two percent of events were rescuers faulted for being insufficiently responsive or responsible.

## Business and Disaster

The private economic sector was usually not mentioned in the response of communities to disaster, but in 14% of cases it was cited as meeting at least some immediate human needs. In two percent of cases it repaired physical damage or restored services such as phone lines. In five percent of cases, however, individuals in the private economic sector were described as exploiting human needs. Even here, the exploiters were likely to be foreign and the circumstances extenuating, as when the French under the Vichy government were reported to have turned to the blackmarket in food to cope with inadequate rations.[43]

Reports that segments of the community are exploiting human needs associated with natural catastrophe are almost non-existent. Only one report of an American catastrophe detailed such opportunistic exploitation. In a Topeka flood of 1903, some merchants were reported to be speculating, buying up potatoes and raising prices. Such conduct was condemned by a "prominent miller" in a manner that enabled The Times to treat it as an aberration: "We do not intend and have never intended to raise the price of flour, no matter what the grocers are thinking of doing."[44]

## The Role of Government

Sixty-five articles, again 18% of the total articles coded, dealt with the role of government in predicting, planning for and coping with disaster. Natural disaster, like war, continuously expanded the sphere of government during the 20th century. Disaster and media disseminated news of disaster helped to justify the expansion of welfare state liberalism and the general liberal position that government is the benevolent instrument of collective social progress. Eventually, the trials of wartime were to show that only government could coordinate and rationalize the effort of the entire society, thus facilitating its survival.

Oceanic travel exposed passengers, investors and insurance companies to natural risks which were compounded by poor shipboard management. When catastrophe occurred, it became imperative to determine which acts were insurable. From 1900 on, *The Times* reported on government commissions of inquiry and carried out its own investigations, interviewing passengers and reconstructing events.

Government officials on the scene during disasters were never found to be unresponsive to human need or insufficiently responsive. This is not to say that government met all immediate human needs. From the point of view of *The Times* it ought not to do so. When floods swept through Kansas and Missouri in 1903, *The Times* editorialized on the role of government in mitigating the effects of natural disaster. Three points were important. Affected populations were expected to make every effort to help themselves. When these efforts were insufficient, state government and outside relief agencies ought to provide supplementary aid at no local cost.

> If the cities which have suffered so heavily want assistance in taking care of their dependent refugees they should have it promptly and freely. It is characteristic of these virile Western cities that they never ask for aid nor accept it so long as they can meet the conditions from their own resources.[45]

For their own part, newspapers were to avoid exaggerated reports of hardship in the interests of sensationalism. By this last criteria, *The Times* found itself to have been responsible in its reporting, in contrast to some "hysterical local newspapers."

In the view of *The Times*, care had to be taken to see that the provision of aid to victims did not produce a greater damage, the loss of self-reliance. War, especially World War II, confused prior notions of local self-reliance in disaster. The World War II period provided the largest percentage of articles in which the focus was on the responsibility of government for mitigating natural disaster. The government's claim on material and moral resources, justified by the war effort, resulted in enhanced expectations by citizens. In setting prices, rationing food and deploying labor, government had deprived localities of the means to cope with social disruption. If the entire civic realm was explicitly or potentially mobilized into the war effort, then government resources could be claimed for civilian problems.

The natural environment as a hazardous context for social activity became less visible during the war. Articles on science dwelt on implications for the war effort. More curiously, those in which nature was a sole and sufficient cause of disruptive events did not occur. This becomes clear in war casualty listings. During World War I, *The Times* printed a running total of the dead and wounded in which "died of disease" was the largest single cause of death.[46] During the last months of the war this category of death was dropped, and it never appeared during the next world conflict. With that war over, the politicization of social life and of science abated, and nature was re-established as an autonomous causal agent.

More recent catastrophes appear to have helped legitimate governments whose ordinary claims to popular support might be tenuous. Nine days after a major earthquake struck Managua, Nicaragua, *The Times* reported that the wife of General Anastasio Somoza Debayle, the nation's military leader, had the coordination of relief efforts well in hand.[47]

## The Bizarre

In forty-seven articles, 13% of the total coded, the overriding emphasis in stories of community and catastrophe was on the bizarre and curious. Events depicted in these were remote from the North American and European concerns of *The Times* or were not considered serious. Such stories entertained, and they acted as a counterpoint both to political and economic news on one hand, and to news about more ordinary natural happenings on the other.

Some bizarre tales could be ominous. For example, in 1903 a Methodist minister wrote to *The Times* to report that the Mexican city of Mazatlan, infected by plague, had been cordoned off by the army and that those who remained now faced famine as well as disease.[48]

These articles could also be about the marvelous. In 1928 a ship captain, taking a load of molasses from Cuba to the United States, found himself caught up in a raging sea. To calm the "mountainous waves" he poured his 70,000 gallon cargo into the water, creating a "stilled area," and saved his ship and crew.[49]

They could even parody familiar weather stories. During a cold spell in 1958 which made the Florida tourist season a catastrophe of sorts, The Times printed a long weather article which satirized the usual formulas. Comedian Joe E. Lewis was described as telling Miami audiences that they should protect themselves against the beach conditions by limiting their exposure to only ten minutes of rain the first day, 15 the second, and so forth.[50]

### Warnings

Warnings about impending weather episodes comprise five percent of all surveyed articles. They give voice to a rhetoric of community concern. In a practical sense, they are usually useless, being imprecise or after-the-fact. One typical example read, "All communities in the bay region are liable to have a real earthquake at any time and should take reasonable precautions to protect life and property."[51]

### Conclusion

The Times' reports on nature are an integral part of the liberal historical perspective evident in the newspaper as a whole. Coverage of the natural world both conforms to the tenets of the liberal ideology and acts as a secondary narrative flow compensating for historical periods in which the political and economic news cannot independently sustain a progressive interpretation of events.

Three premises are evident in The Times' coverage of natural events. First, scientific inquiry has a progressive quality which reduces apparent natural chaos to comprehensible and predictable order. To some degree, not merely protection against but control of the natural environment is or will be possible. The state plays a central role in underwriting and coordinating scientific research for the general welfare.

Second, while the scientific enterprise is cumulative and owes much to teamwork, individual curiosity and risk-taking are essential for progress—good science is a vehicle for individualism. Similarly and by implication, a good newspaper can also be scientific if its editors remain objective and its reporters are willing to exercise initiative and face danger in tracking down the truth.

Third, the disruptive potential of nature is mitigated by the moral solidarity and heroism which localities display in responding to emergencies—natural disasters provide newsworthy evidence of the pervasiveness of moral community in the modern world.

The consequences of *The Times'* nature and disaster coverage containing these premises are threefold. First, *The Times* is able to articulate an historically prior system of community-based values. Its notions of community correspond to the neighborly responsibility of the old middle class of the small town rather than reflect the mobility expectations and social suspicion of a newer middle class. By their occupations and careers, this strata is tied to bureaucratic affiliations rather than to locality, and resides in the metropolis rather than the town. But this new middle class is the primary audience for *The Times*. By extolling values no longer operational with this class, the newspaper enables urbanites to maintain a collective reverence for them nonetheless, and so marks the moral boundaries of a national community of the imagination. The ritual similarity evident in coverage of natural catastrophe involves *The Times'* readers in a mediated experience of community concern. Such stories are emotionally compelling as drama without requiring an obligatory and practical response. Like tornadoes in the recollection of childhood, these are once-removed disasters, community-confirming and reassuring. Readers are ceremonially involved in a nostalgic image of community which can co-exist with and facilitate life within a more instrumental everyday world.

Second, *The Times'* reporting celebrates and justifies two central themes of liberalism: faith in human progress through science and the conviction that such progress requires an activist and expanding role for government. This role, in turn, legitimates state perogatives necessary to rationalize social benevolence. The coordination of research by the state and governmental intervention in times of disaster have become liberal expectations, inplicit in *The Times'* coverage. Total war, like a particularly virilent plague, legitimates the most complete mobilization of civic resources by the state.

The publicity given to the scientific conquest of nature and to the remedial activity of the welfare state have simultaneously highlighted the failings of these endeavors. These failings have, in turn, cast doubt on the liberal program for the state. *The Times*, as a result, has had to temper its commitment to progress through the natural and social sciences. Since the early 1950s, it has run feature stories in which nature successfully evades unlimited human manipulation. Some things—swine flu, innoculation, the artificial heart, a space-based laser defense—may not be worth accomplishing. Indeed, they may bring unanticipated grief.

Rather than openly repudiating liberalism and its central role for the state in social welfare and scientific endeavor, *The Times* has adopted an ambivalent stance. Here it affirms the utopian promise of science, there it advocates prudently working within the limits of human nature and the natural world. It is as though the urban new middle class, the newspaper's primary readership, has lost its grounds for historic optimism without as yet being able to fabricate a post-liberal metaphor through which to understand its future as a class, the national society, or the state.

## Notes

1. Ferdinand de Saussure, *Course in General Linguistics* (New York: McGraw-Hill, 1966). p. 117.
2. Ibid.
3. Alfred Schutz, *On Phenomenology and Social Relations,* H. R. Wagner. (Chicago: The University of Chicago Press, 1970). p. 80.
4. Karl Mannheim, *Ideology and Utopia* (New York: Harcourt, Brace & World, 1936).
5. Ibid, p. 226.
6. Gardening news combines weather forecasts with practical advice. The latter would seem to anchor metropolitan residents in the enduring certainties of nature. "Poison Ivy: Use aerosol preparations to control this unwanted vine . . . Fruit Trees: Spray again with a general purpose formula to protect developing fruit from maggots and diseases. *The New York Times* (hereafter abbreviated *NYT*), July 8, 1985, p. B7. Editorial page celebration of the changing seasons, a regular *Times* feature, is further evidence of the newspaper's interest in rooting the social environment in a broader and more cyclically stable natural context.
7. *NYT,* Sept. 4, 1928, p. 2.
8. *NYT,* Nov. 21, 1933, p. 1
9. *NYT,* Dec. 12, 1938, p. 1.
10. *NYT,* Aug. 26, 1968, p. 77.

11. See for example, "Sea's Grim Toll of Fifty Years," *NYT*, Oct. 12, 1913, p. 3.
12. The method employed by *The Times* in contextualizing loss provides a script to the general public similar to that spontaneously adopted in personal experience of heavy snowfall or exceptionally cold temperature. People boast about the adversity. If it can be related to a record, so much the better for communicating both the problem and the fact that people have survived.
13. *NYT*, Oct. 4, 1908, Part 5, p. 5.
14. Ibid.
15. "Sixty Innoculated in Test," *NYT*, March 6, 1918, p. 8.
16. "Tests of Vaccine to Stop Influenza," *NYT*, Oct. 4, 1918, p. 10.
17. "Malaria Scourge Fought by TVA," *NYT*, Apr. 23, 1938, p. 7.
18. Marriage announcements featured the relationship of the bridegroom and sometimes the bride to the war effort. Newsprint supply was fixed by Order L-240, instituted in late 1942, at each newspaper's 1941 newsprint consumption. Meyer Berger, *The Story of The New York Times 1851-1951* (New York: Simon and Schuster, 1951), p. 476.
19. "Synthetic Biotin, 'Life' Vitamin, Is Achieved After Long Research," *NYT*, May 18, 1943, p. 9.
20. "U. S. Army Starts London Vice Fight," *NYT*, June 2, 1943, p. 9.
21. "Presence of Cholera in Rome Verified," *NYT*, Sept. 4, 1973, p. 2.
22. "Scientists Find Virus They Believe May Cause Transfusion Hepatitis," *NYT*, June 17, 1978, p. 1.
23. Supplementary material from *The New York Times* News Service and the Associated Press, by Henry Kamm, available from *The New York Times* only on microfilm because the paper was not publishing on this date due to a labor strike.
24. Meyer Berger, *NYT*, p. 275.
25. Berger, *NYT*, p. 346.
26. Berger, *NYT*, p. 254.
27. *NYT*, Jan. 1, 1913, p. 12.
28. Berger, *NYT*, pp. 283, 339.
29. Berger, *NYT*, pp. 62-67.
30. Berger, *NYT*, pp. 488-89.
31. Former managing editor Turner Cateldge calls these stories "journalistic adventure [that] seized the world's imagination." Turner Cateldge, *My Life and The Times* (New York: Harper & Row, 1971), p.291.
32. "Two Polio Victims Win Vaccine Suit But Cutter Is Held Not Negligent," *NYT*, Jan. 18, 1958, p. 1.
33. *NYT*, Nov. 14, 1963, p. 1.
34. *NYT*, April 15, 1973, p. 1.
35. "Record Bubonic Plague Outbreak Makes New Mexico's Pet Owners Wary," *NYT*, Aug. 22, 1983, p. 14.
36. "85 Are Killed In Georgia Tornado," *NYT*, June 2, p. 1.
37. "Big Storm In The South," *NYT*, Oct. 3, 1898, p. 1.
38. "Austrian Cabinet Crisis," *NYT*, June 22, 1918, p. 1.
39. "Yellow Fever In Mexico Is Now Beyond Control," *NYT*, Nov. 16, 1903, p. 1.
40. "12 Lives Are Lost In Quebec Floods," *NYT*, Sept. 2, 1938, p. 19.
41. Ibid.
42. "Disaster Off Gay Head," *NYT*, Dec. 2, 1898, p. 1.
43. "Hunger In France Preys On Children," *NYT*, Aug. 21, 1943, p. 11.
44. Ibid. "Topeka's New Peril," *NYT*, June 2, 1903, p. 2.
45. "The Western Floods," *NYT*, June 2, 1903, p. 8.
46. *NYT*, April 11, 1918, p. 1.
47. Marvine Howe, "Mrs. Somoza Runs Much Of Quake Relief," *NYT*, Jan. 1, 1973, p. 5.
48. "Horrors Of Mazatlan," *NYT*, Jan. 25, 1903, p. 1.

49. "Sea Calmed By Molasses," *NYT*, Jan. 23, 1928, p. 21.
50. Paul J. C. Friedlander, "Jet Stream Winter," *NYT*, Feb. 16, 1958, p. 2E.
51. Professor Bailey Willis, quoted in "Sharp Earthquake Felt In San Francisco; Los Angeles, Hours Later, Has Another," *NYT*, Jan. 1, 1933, p. 3.

# Public Icons and Bourgeois Novels
## Cultural Expressions in Francoist Spain

**Aurelio L. Orensanz**

## Introduction

This paper is based on research of a phenomenon of mass culture as it developed in Spain during the sixties and seventies. Throughout those decades, a group of graphic artists, photographers, and advertising executives, under the supervision of a core team of bureaucrats, published 320 tourist posters for the *Dirección General de Promoción del Turismo* (General Office of Tourist Promotion) of the *Ministerio de Información y Turismo* (Ministry of Information and Tourism). That collection of posters, together with other promotional programs, triggered one of the most successful tourist campaigns ever, making Spain the first tourist destination for European tourists. The number of tourists visiting Spain jumped from 6,100,000 in 1960, to 24,100,000 in 1970, and to 49,500,000 in 1980. Tourism became Spain's largest industry, generating an income of $297 million in 1960, $1.6 billion in 1970, and $3.7 billion in 1980, precipitating the industrialization of the country and its modernization. To accomplish this a new image of Spain had to be articulated; one that would, first, neutralize decades of ill feelings harbored by the industrial masses throughout Europe, and then seize the imagination and fantasy of these masses.

Our contention is that those 320 posters are not only a collection of discrete pieces of information, unrelated and fragmentary, but a body of images and texts formed by a coherent system of verbal and visual codes. They were not intended primarily as an ideological outlet for the dissemination of political rhetoric nor as a carrier of official propaganda. They were brought about as a piece-meal production over the course of some 20 years, and were conceived and used strictly as tourism advertising materials. But, in spite of that primary promotional objective, they were inscribed with a stylistic unity and a conceptual coherence that makes them fertile soil from which to retrieve a symbolic universe and a world view of Spain. This collection of tourist posters appears as the

The International Journal of Politics,
Culture and Society, 1(2), Winter 1987    52 [242]

most consistent and embracing production of mass communication ever put forward by any official agency of the Francoist regime which ruled for 40 years.

We here try to reconstruct the image of Spain deposited in those posters; just as fingerprints supply evidence of one's identity, those posters supply evidence of a political discourse. Our aim is to uncover a consistent language concealed behind those glossy advertisements.[1]

The contours of this language are more apparent when seen in the context of a regime that tightly controlled the production and circulation of all forms of public language and discourse. The task of exercising rigorous, ruthless control over the production and dissemination of any form of public discourse was given to the same Ministry of Information and Tourism.

The state, through the Ministry of Information and Tourism, enforced a strict censorship over the press, radio, television and newspapers, while creating its own network of newspapers, radio and television stations, publishing concerns, and even motion picture studios. State movie production failed irreversibly by the early fifties, and the State press, radio and publishing agencies never really made an impact, since the public overwhelmingly favored privately controlled media. The state concentrated on promoting its own television system and in curbing freedom of other media.[2] Comparatively speaking, among those involved with these media, writers and publishers of fiction got a somewhat freer hand. Somehow the Ministry of Information and Tourism considered books as a medium that implied private consumption, addressed to the cultured and more restricted segments of Spanish society. This would make possible an outpouring of novels, short stories, and travel books, as well as novelists. These new generations of novelists were considered to be bearers of a national critical consciousness and, as such, would be able to attain a significant status in the Spanish society of the fifties and sixties. Their books, clad and disguised in the techniques and resources of their own genres, would supply a counterpoint to official rhetoric.

We will examine some of those books because they provide the fertile soil from which to retrieve a functional counter-discourse, and counter-language, to the official rhetoric of the tourist posters. Since Spanish contemporaneous movies of the fifties and sixties, and early seventies are patterned after the same social, political, and aesthetic molds of the novels, we could have used a sample of them to build up the countermodel of the political discourse of the posters. However, these movies are a visual medium, and their repression by the censor of the Ministry of Information and Tourism was so unremitting and ruthless, that they were put in a very disadvantageous position when compared to that of the fiction being published. Cinema, in comparison to literature, was not perceived as an elitist and minority product, but as an all-out mass medium, addressed to the heterogenous popular masses, who were overwhelmingly made up of working class illiterate people. Finally, the realism of the photographic image, with its capacity to influence the behavior of the young and the uneducated, was deemed dangerous compared to that of any other mass medium.

The novels contain an alternative symbolic universe, or a countersymbolic universe to the one developed in the corpus of the Spanish tourist posters. They develop a universe of crude realism, pessimism, economic deprivation, and the social inequalities prevalent in Spanish society. The language in which it is conveyed, for the most part, is one of realism, with characters and situations passionately depicted with engrossing dialogue, and with abundant use of metonymy and synecdoche and other technical devices, all of which serve to involve the reader and make him an aware and active participant.

A sample of some relevant Spanish novels of the fifties, sixties and seventies will be used, then, as a comparison to the official discourse of the tourist posters, as a counterpoint to the State language as portrayed in the posters.

## Selective Visual and Textual Images of Spain

The vast and diversified array of images that make up Spanish tourist posters can be roughly divided into two main categories: those of culture and those of nature. Posters of cultural content include 172 units (54% of the total), and posters of nature include 139 units (44% of the total). The remaining 2%, nine units, consist of varying themes.

As we will see, culture and nature are perceived and presented in Spanish tourist posters with very specific qualifications. In the category of culture we include 74 units that portray works of art which include paintings, sculpture, jewelry, illuminated manuscripts, mosaics, stained glass, inscriptions, architecturally significant buildings, bridges, and the like. They are, for the most part, pieces of cultural import, landmarks, and stereotypes of the national heritage—a "parthenon of best-sellers" as T. W Adorno would put it. There are another 19 posters of tourist inns, a state-owned and managed network of hotels housed in old castles and other historic structures which have been refurbished by the additions of modern facilities and services, and decorated with antiques and other items of classical taste. Our category of culture is finally completed by 27 more posters that depict the spirit and values of the country through the use of close-ups of door-knockers, roof-tops and emblematic animals. To the same category must be added five more posters that, in the body of this chapter, are classified as posters of cultural consumption.

The block of 139 posters depicting scenes from nature is made up of 97 posters that present impressive vistas of the Spanish countryside and its coastlands. Here we include two other groups of posters: those on climatic themes (31 units) and those on geographic themes (11 units). Culture and nature, then, are the two main hinges upon which Spanish tourist posters derive their universe of meaning.

The process of making the posters took place over a 20-year period, with a core team of three or four men working in close collaboration on the selection of the images and their graphic design. They were helped by four graphic designers and some eighty photographers with varying degrees of involvement. To begin with, assignments were made on very general themes. The photographers first too] pictures in certain areas and then returned them to the designer and the directing team, presenting them with many shots. Th designers and the directing team then selected the photograph which were to be made into posters. Next came the process selecting the text to accompany the image, which was done l an ongoing interaction between graphic designers and the directir team.

On the basis of first-hand information from many of these me we know that they never worked within a rigid conceptu framework, in terms of aesthetics, ideology, or systematic conte Thus, the thematic distribution of the Spanish tourist posters not result from a preconceived plan, but from an instinctual, s imposed set of operational criteria. Over a 20-year period, a ser of themes consistently recurred in this collection, themes that l not been imposed from outside. The core team responsible for production of these posters generated an ideology that apparent, that was built into all official outlets, and that reinforced from the top to bottom of the administration, though with very few explicit formulations. Francoism produced very few works which can be classified either as visual or performing art, nor did it produce many novels, films or even much music of its own. It is probably to the tourist poster that we can turn for the most fertile ground from which to retrieve objective traces and remains of Francoism.

The tourist poster objectivizes a world view that is optimistic, reassuring, and assertive in its tone. It is one-directional, patronizing and imposing in its format. Spanish tourist posters make a statement about a world without conflicts and tensions. The images and forms presented of labor, leisure, arts and crafts are mostly pre-industrial; of an idealized nature, and of rural lifestyles, domestic and homely; and of communal forms of association and communication. The only activities shown are related to alien tourists. In a word, it is a world of a classless society, disassociated from the historic pressures and frictions of any time and space.

It is a regressive discourse because of its content, namely, the negation of the present. However, it is also a progressive one because of its goals and format. It embraces modern technology wholeheartedly, making it part of its language and message. To bring about that complex marriage successfully, some major stylistic steps had to be taken. We will see this marriage through two foci: the reinterpretation of the rural world and the use of religious themes, the two centerpieces of traditional Spain.

The rural world has been captured in several dozen posters. Three of the most relevant are posters that depict rooftops. They are close-ups of rooftop tiles. These posters transmit, first and foremost, information about traditional rural architecture; small sized buildings, rough and outdated construction materials, small villages, closeness of the houses, etc. At the same time the connotations of those rooftops could easily be read by the audiences both abroad and at home as conveying feelings of close knit relations, harmony, environmental integrity, immersion in nature, mutual and direct support, austere, modest and unpretentious lifestyles, disciplined, orderly and undemanding expectations.

It was precisely during the early sixties, and through the middle seventies, that close to two million farmers left their villages for the industrial slums of West Germany, France, The Netherlands, Belgium, and Switzerland. Hundreds upon hundreds of villages became depopulated and deserted. Besides the two million Spanish farmers who went abroad, another two million settled in cities such as Madrid, Barcelona, Bilbao, Zaragoza, and Valencia. There was no central industrial and economic planning of any kind for farmers. The distribution of land, and related problems of land use and tenure, age old political and economic issues, ceased to exist from that time on. Education, health and public administration services were drastically cut in the countryside. Spanish rural life passed through its bleakest period. Ironically enough, the farmers displaced to the industrial slums of Spain and abroad served the national industrial and economic plans like no other economic force, except tourists. During the short period from 1960 through 1966, the workers who had emigrated to Europe remitted to Spain money orders worth $144 million.[3]

It is during this period that Spanish tourist posters swept the country, Europe, and for that matter, all the industrial West with icons of the rural world elaborated and tailored to picture the pure, the authentic, the relaxing, and the cult of the primitive. For the urban middle class masses this aesthetic interpretation of the rural world meant the end of centuries old complaints. For the recently immigrated, uprooted masses of the Spanish slums the rural icons would constitute, through aesthetics, an *a posteriori* vindication of their harsh but noble origins. Tourist posters would contribute to spur and foster a cult of the rural. For the urban masses of age old industrial Europe, such as Germany, The Netherlands, Belgium, Great Britain, and Northern France, the tourist image of rural Spain would make accessible a glimpse at the roots, the rural values of pre-reformed, colorful Europe.

What tourist posters give us is visual evidence of the rural, sliced away, and cut off from everything else. The power of the Spanish tourist poster was its visual synecdoche or visual rhetoric, through which it was capable of dissolving into aesthetics the brunt of an issue by focusing the view of a subject into one of its segments.

Twenty explicitly religious themes appear in our collection of tourist posters. One depicts the Pantocractor of the church of *St. Climent de Tahull*, in the Pyrenees of Lérida, near Andorra. Today it is one of the most revered and highly considered mural Romanesque paintings, held in the collection of the *Museu d'Art Romanic de Catalunya*, in Barcelona. It is a world famous icon because of the perfection of its drawing, and the intensity of the message it conveys: Christ, Lord of the Universe and Judge of History. That poster reproduces only the immediate area of his right eye. What the public sees is a big, staring eye, of Picassian/

Romanesque simplicity, and strength. Its caption asks: "Have you ever seen Spain?"

Religion is a deeply felt subject matter in all quarters of Spanish life. Hardly any other topic is capable of arousing stronger emotions. Religion is a source of identity, and of spiritual and emotional support for large segments of the population. For some others, religion in general, and Catholicism in particular, is associated with backwardness, repression, intolerance and privileges. Conservative Catholicism has been a prominent ingredient of national, traditionalist ideology since the eighteenth century, first against Northern and Central European liberal culture and then against atheistic traditions in socialism and communism. Conversely, very few countries in Europe can show a stronger tradition of anti-clericalism and iconoclasm.

For the skeptical, secularized masses at home and for the industrial masses abroad, the profusion of explicit religious themes could unearth dormant associations of bigotry, superstition, or at least "Un-reformation." To avoid such associations, Spanish tourist posters would neutralize religious images. Religious themes would be removed from their devotional contexts. Through the use of visual synecdoche, meaning would be cropped and sliced. Religious icons would become things beautiful and acceptable to everybody, ingredients of the national heritage, irrespective of centuries old awe and aura associated with them. A dramatically new interpretation of religious artifacts and religion would be induced—a detached, unemotional, and secularizing vision. An ideology of planned economic growth would achieve what the high brow liberalism and church burning revolution of the civil war years unsuccessfully tried to do.

Spanish tourist posters would carry on throughout the sixties and seventies the initial, never fully developed, seminal optimism that the Francoist revolution always lived off of. The Francoist national, syndicalist revolution, always used the slogan *"Por el Imperio hacia Dios"* ("Through the Empire to God"). The exact meaning of this slogan was never clear. Since the Spanish national, syndicalist revolution was never able to develop itself through geographical expansion, as did its Italian and German counterparts, Francoism was forced to live an interior, spiritual expansion. The goals of that expansion would be set on recovering if not the lands at least the world view, the universe of meaning, of the conquerors, discoverers and missionaries of the Gold Century (XVI), of the architects of the consolidation of Spain as one nation

(XV), and of the initiators of the liberation of Christian Spain from Muslim rule in the Middle Ages. The reference to God in the slogan ("Through the Empire to God") added an uplifting theological touch to such a vague program.

These were the boundaries of the political discourse of Francoism and were the ultimate parameters of the discourse of the Spanish tourist posters, as well. In them time would oscillate between nostalgia, and a dream atmosphere; and space would be an inner, spiritualized dimension called Spain.

### The Movement of the Spanish Realist Novel

Contemporaneous with the production of tourist posters was an outpouring of novels from which we will draw for the construction of a parallel language, a language that runs counter to the main themes and format of the posters. We will base our contrast on a series of twelve novels, plus a handful of travel books written by authors of the same generation, some of them novelists. Those novels are: *La Colmena* (The Beehive) by Camilo José Cela (written in 1945 and published in 1950); *Los Bravos* (The Brave Ones) by Jesús Fernández Santos (1954); *El Jarama* (The Jarama) by Rafael Sánchez Ferlosio (1956); *Central Eléctrica* (Electric Plant) by Jesús López Pacheco (1958); *La Piqueta* (The Pickaxe) by Antonio Ferres (1959); *Tiempo de Silencio* (Time of Silence) by Luís Martín Santos (1962); *Dos Días de Septiembre* (Two days of September) by José Caballero Bonald (1962); *Cinco Horas con Mario* (Five Hours with Mario) by Miguel Delibes (1966); *Ultimas Tardes con Teresa* (Last Evenings with Teresa) by Juan Marsé (1966); *Señas de Identidad* (Signs of Identity) by Juan Goytisolo (1966); *Volverás a Región* (You will Return to the Region) by Juan Benet (1967); and *La Saga/ Fuga de J. B.* (The Saga/Escape of J. B.) by Gonzalo Torrente Ballester (1972).

The travel books we will refer to are: *Campos de Níjar* (Fields of Níjar) by Juan Goytisolo (1960); *Caminando por las Hurdes* (Walking around Las Hurdes) by Armando López Salinas and Antonio Ferres (1960); *Tierra de Olivos* (Land of Olive Trees) by Antonio Ferres (1964); *Donde Las Hurdes se llaman Cabrera* (Where Las Hurdes are called Cabrera) by Ramón Carnicer (1964); and *Por el Río Abajo* (Down the River) by Alfonso Grosso (1966).[4]

The above list can be considered a fair representation of the Spanish novel during the years from 1950 to the 1970's. It is not complete and does not cover all the avenues of Spanish fiction. Instead it is a list that encompasses a horizon appropriate to our universe of study. As a matter of fact, thousands of new titles were written during these decades reflecting the socially privileged position the writer has always enjoyed in Spanish speaking countries. Since in Spain the usual outlets of reflection and social criticism, such as social research and publication, teaching, and civic involvement, were practically closed, only the veiled formats of poetry, fiction and, to some extent, Theological discourse, were permitted. The government monitored most closely television, cinema, and theatre, followed by radio, and the daily press. Fiction publishing could operate under more flexible reins, allowing the realist novel to develop its own themes.

The time span of our sample of novels is not symmetric with the period encompassed by the posters. The posters cover the entire sixties and most of the seventies, while our sample of novels starts in the fifties and extends into the seventies. From the mid-forties on, realism becomes a growing and pervading tenet not only in the novel but in poetry, theatre and cinema. In spite of the stronger censorship exerted on playwrights and filmakers than on novelists and poets, there was a crop of plays and movies that helped establish realism as the common ground of aesthetics by the early fifties. The artists responsible for the production of the Spanish tourist posters have stressed that their aesthetic, rhetorical and structural world crystallized once and for all in the early sixties. The realist aesthetics of the posters appears stylistically, as another chapter of the Spanish realism of that time.

In the fifties a new generation of writers appear on the literary scene conscious of the weight of the Civil War and its ramifications. They do not belong to either the winning or losing party, rather it is their parents that do. They have rebelled, and have decided to break with the current literary scene. Novels such as *Nada* (1945) by Carmen Laforet and *La Colmena* (1951) by Camilo José Cela are worlds apart from the new perspective, since such works were purely subjective, defensive and in the long run evasive of reality. The main characteristic of this new breed of writers was to relate the truth as they saw it to ensure that the general public, otherwise systematically denied reliable information about Spanish life, would be accurately appraised of their society.

This commitment to literary realism cannot be linked to any specific political ideology and, even less, did not lead to an identification of their aesthetic tenets with those of Soviet socialist realism. In fact, neither *Los Bravos* (1954) by Jesús Fernández Santos, or *El Jarama* (1956) by Rafael Sánchez Ferlosio, or the first novels by Juan Goytisolo reveal a clear political ideology. However, their position is left-wing, in opposition to the regime. Although they are politically confused, they render an accurate analysis of what is going on in Spain. They depart sharply from the purely personal and aesthetic distance maintained by their predecessors.

But when we come to a book such as *Central Eléctrica* (1958) by Armando López Salinas, or *Campos de Níjar* (1960) by Juan Goytisolo, the existence of a political ideology, and even of some party allegiances appears very clearly. *Central Eléctrica* espouses ideas that bear a striking resemblance to socialist realism, in the specific and technical sense of the term. We cannot say that there is an inevitable tendency to go from social critique to political partisanship and that therefore *El Jarama* and *La Mina* are both the beginning and the end of the same line, but we certainly can say that they share a common ground and that they take a realist approach to social reality in Spain.

Most of those who authored works which we include in this category were born between 1922 and 1936, though there are some from the previous generation, including Luís Romero, Angel María de Lera and Suárez Carreño. During the fifties, when this group began to write, Spain was reentering the international arena. She became a member of such international bodies as the United Nations and UNESCO, entered into agreements with the United States, and made a concordat with the Holy See. Her income began to rise as she began to experience affluence from abroad.

Significant numbers of Spaniards began to travel outside of Spain and the bureau of censorship made allowances that only a few years before would have been unthinkable.

This new generation looked to Europe and compared what they saw at home with what they saw abroad. For the most part, they came to the conclusion that there were structural deficiencies which pervaded the Spanish social fabric. They did not take sides either with the generation of older writers who lived through the war and interpreted Spain accordingly, nor with the exile writers who left the country and lamented the course of events which resulted in their exile. This new generation wanted to measure the present Spain of the fifties and early sixties against its European counterparts. For them the culprit became the establishment. These writers became known as the "new generation of 98." They showed a deep dissatisfaction with their country, and yet looked for the essence of the true and ideal Spain in order to overcome their alienation, as opposed to the writers of the sixties who dealt with the Spain of the here-and-now.

The "new generation of 98" saw themselves first and foremost as writers, as fiction writers with the secondary mission to reflect upon the social and political situation of the country, something that the press had not done for years. The goals of these writers were to convey areas of social concern, through fiction writing, and to achieve a much needed freedom of expression. Their efforts engendered a climate of dissent and the objective quality of their work enabled them to convince their readers that Spain indeed had stagnated and, accordingly, was unfit for life in modern times.

The thread that binds together these generations of writers and literary thrusts is a full scale exploitation of surrounding reality. Page after page in their works we see a stunning directness with which things and words are recorded, and an obsession with the flow of time that envelops the things and events described.

A denotative narrative technique conveys the totality of a situation through the selection of extremely precise details. The following is a passage from *Central Eléctrica*. El Cholo, a rapist, is going to encounter La Manuela, who is waiting for him in a barn. Two dogs are playing, and although we are given the sounds and sights of things, we never know exactly what happens. The account of the action is so thoroughly physical, documentary and ambiguous that we do not know if it is of the dogs or of El Cholo and La Manuela:

> El Cholo is no longer at the door of the barn. The straw rustles; flies hover around; a hen heads quickly to the door of the barn, and stands there still, in the rectangle of the afternoon sun that peeps through the door, bending its neck, staring at something; the pigs outside grunt fearful of the dogs; all the cows are lying on the ground and one smoothly pushes its calf with its snout; the smell of so many animals mixed with the vapor of their breath; and the rustle every time louder of the crushing straw; the flies are hitting the bellies of the cows desperately. The barn is a dense mixture of sounds, low and continuous sounds, silent, restless; the straw smells of manure, the dirty life; everything is sticky and hot, due perhaps to the last rays of sun that penetrate the door of the barn.[5]

This information is given with the directness of a camera or a tape recorder, no less faithfully than the pictures of our posters. In another example, taken from *Tiempo de Silencio*. Luís Martín

Santos describes a frustrating conversion between Dorita and a police officer of the local precinct. Only the words of the police officer are quoted. Dorita's words are not recorded, her anxiety, frustration and defenselessness are thoroughly conveyed:

— Who do you want?
— No, you cannot.
— What is your relationship to him?
— No, you cannot talk to him.
— Don't worry, young lady. In the end, everything will be all right. Believe me. And I have seen everything in my life.
— No, you cannot send him a message.
— No, it is not that bad.
— No one can be seen for 72 hours.
— Yes, 72 hours.
— Who told you that?
— He has been here for three hours.
— No, I don't know that.
— Don't worry.
— Take it easy, and go to bed.
— Don't make a scene.
— I am telling you that it is impossible, that it was impossible.
— I wish I could.
— You are welcome.
— Absolutely impossible.
— Of course, you can come back tomorrow.
— What is your name again?[6]

As with the posters, this narrative was never purely denotative, and only assumed connotative overtones as it progressed. Denotation and connotation always go hand in hand, although in differing degrees. Even those authors whose work most closely reflects reality, still endow their prose with meaning and intention. Very often, that intention is conveyed through the use of humor. Irony abounds in Juan Marsé; sarcasm in Ana María Matute; scorn to the point of cruelty in Luís Martín Santos; playful and sour psychological caricature in Delibes; and black humor of a Goyan nature in Juan Benet.

Very often, authors establish a dialectical tension in the development of their characters. Delibes confronts Mario's and Carmen's opinions, goals, and aspirations. Juan Marsé counterposes the idealization that bourgeois Teresa has forged of the slum, El Carmelo, in Barcelona, with the vision that proletarian Pijoaparte has of a residential neighborhood. Juan Benet overlaps and counterpresents play and war, in a tragic superimposition, in his *Volverás a Región*. And Luís Martín Santos employs a dialectical technique to analyze and address the paralyzed lifestyles and values of the Spanish people.

If in terms of denotation and connotation we see a lack of parallelism between posters and novels, when addressing the semiotic concept of inventory and story the diversion is complete. Posters are devoid of a visible subject or subjects who can organize the elements of the picture around them; novels, on the other hand, are full of them. In some cases, the subject is an entire segment of the population, such as the lower middle class in *La Colmena*; a group of middle class youngsters in *El Jarama*; and the affluent, cultured young generation of *Señas de Identidad*. The travel books, as well, base their descriptive material on people, and delight in the affairs of people. Whether it is a mass of people as in *La Colmena* or an individual, as in *Señas de Identidad*, people fill up and even overflow from the pages of Spanish realist narratives. People are alienated, disappointed, repressed, uncertain, uncommitted, lustful, unattractive, deformed, resentful, desperate, blasphemous, enraged, vindictive, passionate . . . just the opposite of the way they appear in our posters. In our novels everything and anything is brought in to stress, to reaffirm and to convey the psychic experience of its characters. From a landscape, to a storm, to the appearance of frying pans and the sight of a church building— everything is there to elaborate on the human experience. In sum, novels are totally based on story, whereas posters are based on inventory.

The concept of story vs. repertory inplies the definition of a time and a space for the story. Time and space are consequently framed in opposite ways in posters and novels. The icons of the tourist posters take a consistent and deliberate jump into the past. In our posters we are taken back into the remote world of classical imageries, and into the indefinable poetic time of landscapes and nature. In the first case, when dealing with art, we are not dealing with the art of a precise segment of the past, say a specific century or a cluster of centuries, but an assortment of artifacts and of things past, that range from about two thousand to some hundred years ago, just short of the industrial revolution. That time line is not crossed, or if the objects do happen to come closer to the contemporary world, as would be the case with Gaudi, then they appear to be endowed with qualifications associated with aura and antiquity. The present or the contemporary does not exist in our posters' cultural themes. When we are offered posters of nature and landscape our perception is on the cosmic, the ageless. Even when people appear to be engaged in sports and enjoying nature, the accent seems to be on the atemporal, pleasurable dimension of the embracing environs. In a few words, Spanish tourist posters are not iconically arranged around an organizing verb, a threading action, or through a moving temporality.

Novels and travel books, on the contrary, are constructed around a tight, gripping, passionate sense of the present. *El Jarama* takes place in the course of 16 hours, from 8:45 AM on a Sunday until 12:50 the following morning, and throughout the narration there are continuous references to time on the lips of its characters. *Dos Días de Septiembre* takes place on the 2nd and 3rd of September, starting early the morning of the first day and ending at midnight of the second. *Cinco Horas con Mario* unfolds during the five hours of Mario's wake and focuses on his wife, colleagues, and neighbors. *Señas de Identidad* happens over three intense days. In *Central Eléctrica* we witness the breakdown of a reservoir. The account is sprinkled, from sentence to sentence, with references to the time. Every twenty minutes a simultaneity of events covering the experience of the community is narrated. As the moment of the explosion gets closer, the action is related by the minute. A sensory description of the events substitutes for their logical perception.

## Political Discourse in Novels and Posters

Spain's civil war was fought not only with guns, but with posters as well. During the war, the entire country was wallpapered by the "paper armies," as poster makers were called. The Republican Government's cause, and the Spanish Revolution in general, inspired hundreds of artists to engage in an amazingly prolific and combative poster blitz. Basically, these posters were designed in a manner totally different from that of the tourist posters of the sixties and seventies.

The Spanish Republican War poster was always centered around virile, disciplined proletarian faces staring frontally at the reader/passerby, and engaging him in eye contact. It was a crusade for involvement: "Join the draft;" "What have you done for victory?" "Farmers, the land is yours;" and "First, let us win the war." The central iconic message and the verbal message were supplemented by a multiplicity of clenched fists, muscular arms, strong hands and other proletarian imageries.

The Spanish Republic War poster contained very little photography. Its iconic and graphic vocabulary was a poor substitution for that of the Russian constructivists and supremacists, duly corrected by the tenets of the mandatory socialist realism, European proletarian culture, and even of German Nazism.[7]

Posters and novels had a similar formal structure during the fifties and early sixties. The posters maintained the same formal and aesthetic structure during the late sixties and the seventies, but the novel introduced new formal and thematic itineraries as civil freedoms were slowly permitted on Spanish territory. The formal structure now consisted of a common interest, the realistic portrayal of Spanish culture. That all should know Spain as it really is, was their ultimate goal, which they attempted to achieve through the realistic techniques of visual and verbal reproduction.

Their common formal structures diverged during the late sixties and early seventies, more ostensibly manifesting two contending and disparate world views. The accurate visual descriptions of our posters are devoid of people; they are stages on which no action and no drama of any kind take place. Both cultural as well as natural images give a proto-image of Spain, unpolluted, preindustrial, before the degradation of mass production and mass consumption, almost before the degradation of human contact. Irrespective of whether or not it is Madrid or Las Hurdes, we are offered an atemporal space, where contradictions, if they existed at all, have been resolved. We are given only one space: Spain. When that space becomes concrete or specific, as in a coastland, a locality, or a village, it fits into that general image as further enticement, as a legendary resonance, an exotic verbal ingredient of that fabulous realm that is Spain. As a global metaphor, posters are talking about a people who are frank, warm, sincere, dignified, gentle, strong . . .

Posters also present a discourse loaded with denotation, inventory and representation. A discourse that is closed, domineering, imperative; an authoritarian language. Posters promise a timeless enjoyment in the specific period of the Spain of a planned economy. Theirs is a message of evasion and diversion from the present and its harsh realities. Posters are couched in a form and content that are at the service of a discourse which is thoroughly optimistic. After all, it is the expression of a regime that was born with the expectation of bringing about a classless revolution, whose world was precisely constructed out of the past.

The novels and travel books of our sample present a picture of the entire country, of its culture and nature. But that culture and nature are merely the reflection and the setting of the repression, the anomie and the alienation of a people. Space is sensed and perceived through the desparate lives of the people who inhabit it. In this sense, there is no difference between life as depicted in the fiction of the early sixties and in the novel of the late sixties. The more the novel moves from the realist format, the more sour and condemnatory its authors become. The novels depict men and women who are confused and alienated, toiling and exploding— sufferings which are manifested by malice, illicit sex and boredom.

The discourse of the novels and travel books of Spain's late fifties, sixties and early seventies objectivizes a world view that is pessimistic, distrustful and seminal in its tone; and multidirectional, subverting, and thought-provoking in its format. For the Spanish realist novels and travel books, Spain is a mire of conflicts and tensions. People labor and live under primitive, and oppressive conditions. Their leisure shows spiritual emptiness and boredom. Novels and books conclude that nothing had changed in spite of the bloody toll of a recent civil war and a quarter of a century of constraint and strict discipline. Class confrontation erupts, or will erupt suddenly. It is a discourse bound by a close, gripping experience of the immediate present and the immediate place. The authors confront their readers with barely concealed falsehood and misery. This is a critical discourse since it disects the asymmetries and contradictions between the proclaimed tenets and everyday experience.

Potentially this is a progressive discourse since it carries the seeds of cathartic self-analysis and awareness; but it is also a regressive discourse since it distrusts modern technology, urban and industrial planning, immigration and tourism, mass communication media, foreign influence, particularly American, and industrial society as a whole.

The progressiveness of the novels resides in their thorough analysis of the Spanish people as an ensemble of different and opposed forces. It is an attempt to create a narrative at the service of the proletarian classes, rejecting the costumbrista approach of the past. It is narrative that draws from various traditions of realism: E. Hemingway, J. Steinbeck, J. Dos Passos, Sinclair Lewis; the objectivism of the French novel, such as Alain Robbe-Grillet; and the various elements of Spanish realism: Leopoldo Alas, Pérez Galdós, Pío Baroja, and the rest of the Generation of 98. But when drawing from these different sources there seems to be, for the first time in the Spanish narrative, a conscious awareness, not only of serving a specific social class, but of making that class the protagonist of cultural processes. The new narrative invents or adapts numerous devices to apprehend new dimensions and shades of reality. All these writers seem to share a sense of the uniqueness of the times, and of the unique role that the working classes are expected to play in the formulation of the immediate and long term future.

These authors reshaped the traditional discourse of the Spanish novel, not only by discarding their direct presence in the text, but also by a new perception of social events. This new perception embraces a double element: human behavior as an historical event. Time is both an integral dimension of interior and exterior characters' lives and is a defining, determining and meaning-giving factor.

This here and now reality in which human behavior is apprehended appears endowed with an almost metaphysical evil. Novelists see themselves as the prophets of doom and gloom against an inescapable collective disaster unless society takes a dramatically different course of action.

The tourist posters and novels both use a common form of metonymy, visual for posters and verbal for novels. They have a common form, but have different results. Posters take a specific slice of the past and make it the bearer of an atemporal, mythical set of values. Novels take a slice of the present and make it the bearer of universal values that project into the future. In both cases reality is dissolved into preconceived values. Neither posters nor novels present a comprehensive vision and interpretation of a reality. Traditional Spain, as re-enacted in the tourist posters, did not look at reality as if it were fluid and changing. The novels see only the present as an isolated entity, as if it was not part of a long tradition.

## Conclusion

Tourist posters and realist novels present two contending and conflicting images of Spain: each presents an extreme case of the unreconcilable nature of the Spanish soul. Each tells the same story about the same subject at the same time and in the same space, but with totally different scripts.

The posters convey a reassuring message of the new and innovative. They convey a quality of self-confidence. They express an uncompromising return to the essence of Spain with the values of her past, balanced by a gentle embrace of the modern world. The posters are technologically innovative but reactionary in their content. They illustrate the technocratic spirit of the industrial and economic paths on which the country had embarked so successfully at the time. Realist novels projected a disaffected, condemnatory negation of everything official, technological, and public. The novels conveyed the feeling that the only hope for Spain hovered deep down in the hearts of the alienated and oppressed masses.

Tourist posters constitute a public discourse fashioned with an eye to public consumption for use in public places. Short, striking, powerful, fleeting, and easily comprehensible to the masses, tourist posters would create public opinion both at home and abroad. The novel, on the contrary, operates in the intimate silent environment of the reader. The novel nevertheless generates a powerful stream of consciousness among the informed and educated elite. The posters were to encompass the public world, while the written word was to hold the reins on private discourse.

Tourist posters appear in the public arena among an array of commercial advertising, with whom they are contending for attention. Their messages are elusive and their effects are unaccountable. Realist novels push their political vision through the no less blurring veils of literary fiction. The posters claimed dominion over the visual and the symbolic, whereas the realist novels entrenched themselves in the recesses of the language. The apparent, immediate takeover of the visual proved to be frail and transient. In the mid-seventies, the private field of language burst forth into the public arena, with the end of Francoism in all its visible forms.

Spanish tourist posters cannot be considered Francoist art, since there was not such an art with a repertoire of artists, a repertoire of artworks and a stylistic, conceptual and economic framework. As a matter of fact there was not a Francoist aesthetics as such, with a specific doctrine, or minimally consistent world view; there was not even a Francoist doctrine in any other field. Francoism can be defined as a situation and a changing correlation of forces, basically linked by one person sailing through different phases with the aim of surviving them. There was an emerging fascist aesthetics in architecture, fashion, cinema, propaganda and literature of little originality in comparison with the German and Italian fascist aesthetics. The Spanish outgrowth did not survive the forties. Spanish tourist posters, therefore, can probably be considered the most consistent visual materialization of the diffuse conceptual body known as Francoism in its technocratic incarnation.

In these cultural patterns there is a pervasive insistence on nature as a realm of old, glamorous and entrancing images, totally devoid of people and unrelated to the present. There is an ever present message which transforms Spain into a trademark or product of consumption. We have, as well, an overwhelming presence of the sender over the receiver. This end is attained by the exclusive use of realistic photography in which metonymy and synecdoche prevail over metaphor. This is a language that has the characteristics of a closed authoritarian type of discourse.

The official rhetoric and the written texts are dominant over asymetrical areas, namely, public space, and the private realm. The official and private discourses are two conflicting, antagonistic visions of public space and the social texture of society. Tourist images and fiction are estranged and alienated from the complexity of everyday social reality. The official language is alienated from civil society; and the novelists' minds are estranged from political discourse. A stagnant public language conveyed an obsolete image of Spain, and the novelists' images refused to acknowledge all of the State's accomplishments.

In presenting the novels and posters side by side, we feel as if we have joined Sancho Panza and Don Quixote on a journey through modern Spain. The two men constantly present conflicting portrayals of Spain and its people, while the people remain confused and puzzled by the ongoing reality.

## Reference Notes

1. This research was begun five years ago, when Professor José Luís Febas and I undertook the task of conducting a study of Spanish tourist posters for the *Instituto Nacional de Turismo*, a Spanish State agency in Madrid. For a more ample discussion of the subject see "Glossy Images and Sour Texts. The Political Discourse of Spanish Tourist Posters," a doctoral dissertation at the Sociology Department of the Graduate Faculty of the New School for Social Research, New York, 1985. A parallel study on Spanish tourist brochures was published by José Luís Febas, "Semiología del lenguaje turístico. Investigación sobre los folletos españoles de turismo" in *Estudios Turísticos*, No. 57–58, Madrid, 1978.

2.  After a century of alternating periods of liberalization and control on the freedom of expression, the second Spanish Republic (1931-1939) lifted the chronic censorship and curbs on expression. In 1928, a new Law of Press was passed in the Nationalist territory, at the apex of the Civil War, that would establish a tight control over the daily press, its main target, and over all other means of communication such as books, magazines, radio, theatre, shows of all kinds, cinema, cultural events, cultural displays and exhibitions. It remained in effect until 1966 when a new Law of Press and Printed Matter somewhat more flexible, was introduced by the Minister of Information and Tourism, Manuel Fraga Iribarne.

    About freedom of expression in Spain under Franco's regime, see Manuel Fernández Areal, *La libertad de la prensa en España*, Edicusa, Madrid, 1971; Pedro Crespo de Lara, *El Artículo 2*, Prensa Española, Madrid, 1975; Antonio Beneyto, *Censura y Política en los escritores españoles;* Plaza y Janés Editores, Barcelona, 1977, pages 31 to 44; Román Gubern, *La Censura: Función política y ordenamiento jurídico bajo el franquismo (1936-1975)*, Ediciones Península, Barcelona, 1981, pages 217 to 223.

3.  Whereas the active working population of the country remained basically the same from 1950 to 1975, comprising roughly 37-38% of the total population, its sectorial distribution changed drastically:

|                          | 1950  | 1960  | 1970  | 1980  |
|--------------------------|-------|-------|-------|-------|
| Agriculture and Fishing  | 48.8  | 41.3  | 29.2  | 18.9  |
| Industry                 | 25.1  | 31.4  | 38.1  | 44.6  |
| Services                 | 26.1  | 27.3  | 32.7  | 36.5  |
| Total                    | 100.0 | 100.0 | 100.0 | 100.0 |

The technocrats drew up development plans which envisioned the creation of twelve major industrial parks throughout the country, mostly outside traditional industrial regions such as Catalonia and the Basque Country. Aside from the major industrial parks, innumerable sections of the country were established to cater to specific industrial interests, as well as to areas of the country which needed economic relief.

While in 1940, 19% of the population lived in cities with more than 100,000 people, in 1965, that figure rose to 33%, and in 1980, to 53%.

This transfer from agricultural to industrial, from rural to urban, was realized in Spain in less than two decades, in contrast to the traditional model of industrialization and urbanization, such as it was experienced in Great Britain, where the same transfer took a century.

4.  Novels

    Camilo José Cela, *La Comena*, Destino, Barcelona, 1951.
    Jesús Fernández Santos, *Los Bravos*, Destino, Barcelona.
    Rafael Sánchez Ferlosio, *El Jarama*,Editorial Destino, Madrid, 1956.
    Jesús López Pacheo, *Central Eléctrica*,Destino, Barcelona, 1958.
    Antonio Ferres, *La Piqueta*, Destino, Barcelona, 1959.
    Luís Martín Santos, *Tiempo de Silencio*, Seix Barral, Barcelona, 1962.
    José Caballero Bonald, *Dos Días* de Septiembre, Seix Barral, Barcelona, 1962.
    Miguel Delibes, *Cinco Horas con Mario*, Destino, Barcelona, 1966.
    Juan Marsé,*Ultimas Tardes con Teresa*, Seix Barral, Barcelona, 1967.
    Juan Goytisolo, *Señas de Identidad*,Joaquín Mortiz, México, 1966.
    Juan Benet, *Volverás a Región*, Destino, Barcelona, 1967.
    Gonzalo Torrente Ballester, *La Saga/Fuga de J. B.*, Barcelona, Destino, 1972.
    Travel Books

Juan Goytisolo, *Campos de Nijar,* Seix Barral, 1963.
Armando López Salinas and Antonio Ferres.
*Caminando por Las Hurdes,* Seix Barral, Barcelona, 1960
Antonio Ferres, *Tierra de Olivos,* Seix Barral, Barcelona, 1964.
Ramón Carnicer, *Donde las Hurdes se Llaman Cabrera,* Seix Barral, Barcelona, 1964
Alfonso Grosso and Armando López Salinas, *Por el Rio Abajo,* Editions du Globe, Paris, 1960.
      For a critical perspective, both in literary and sociological terms, see the following books:
Pablo Gil Casado, *La Novela Social Española 1942-1968.* Biblioteca Breve de Bolsillo, Editorial Seix Barral, Barcelona, 1968.
J. Butt, *Writers and Politics in Modern Spain,* Hodder and Stoughton, London, 1978.
Edenia Guillermo and Juana Amelia Hernández, *Novelistica Española de los Sesenta;* Eliseo Torres and Sons, New York, 1971.
Carlos Blanco Aguinaga et alii, *Historia Social de la Literatura Española en Lengua Castellana,* III, Editorial Castalia, Madrid, 1979.
Domingo Yndurain, *Historia y Crítica de la Literatura Española, VIII, Epoca Contemporánea 1939-1980,* Editorial Critica, Barcelona, 1980.
5. Jesús López Pacheco, op. cit. pages 19-20.
6. Luis Martín Santos, op. cit. pages 181-182.
7. Comprehensive studies of Spanish Republican and war posters are in Carmen Grimau, *El Cartel Republicano en la Guerra Civil.* Ediciones Cátedra, S. A., Madrid, 1979.
Jaume Miratvilles, Joseph Termes y Carles Fontseré, *Carteles de la República y de la Guerra;* La Gaya Ciencia, Barcelona, 1978.
Valeriano Bozal, *Historia del Arte en España,* Madrid, Itsmo, 1971, specially chapter 24.
Imma Julián "El Cartelismo y la Gráfica en la Guerra Civil en España", in *Vanguardia Artística y Realidad Politica: 1936-1976;* Colec, *Communicación Visual,* Barcelona, Gustavo Gili, 1976.

# From Matrimony to Malaise:
# Men and Women in the American Film, 1930-1980

**Stanford M. Lyman**

## Introduction

Woody Allen had toyed with the idea of entitling his 1976 film
*Annie Hall* "anhedonia," the psychoanalyst's term for an inability
to experience pleasure. That inability is further elaborated in
*Manhattan*, Allen's 1979 film, when the male lead, a television
writer played by Allen himself, dictates an idea for a new scenario:
"People in Manhattan are constantly creating these real
unnecessary neurotic problems for themselves that keep them from
dealing with more terrifying unsolvable problems about the
universe." Whatever the more terrifying insoluble cosmological
problems are, we quickly learn from these two films that
"anhedonia" arises from the unfathomable, worldly, but routine
terrors of sex, love, and death. Although Joan Didion has recently
cautioned against taking Allen's basic idea too seriously—she holds
that it is not much more than a pseudo-sophisticated, overaged,
adolescent's smug attempt at cuteness[1]—the issues cannot be so
easily dismissed. Allen's recent films are usually regarded as time-
bound and unique, concerned with the stresses and tensions
affecting the personal and social lives of educated, middle-class
professionals living in New York City; however, they express the
deeper theme of the relations of the sexes, a theme that has been
depicted in American films for the past four decades. "Anhedonia"
names a powerful, undefined *dis-ease* that affects the relations
between American men and women. However, its exposure in

---

* Revised version of a paper presented at the annual meeting of the Modern
Language Association, San Francisco, 1979. I am indebted to the helpful
comments of Arthur J. Vidich, Charles Simpson, and Cecil Greek.

73 [263]

cinematic consciousness could only occur after films had cleared away the ideological cover that shielded it from direct perception.

"Anhedonia" speaks to a deep and unresolved dilemma in the American *Lebenswelt*. In its penultimate form it expresses itself as a frenzied desire to escape coupled with a recognition that there is no place to go. Nothing is left but sudden, sharp, uncathartic aggressive displays, and then—ultimately—a grudging acquiescence to a life alternating between boredom and frustration.

American films of the last four decades provide data for uncovering popular expressions of this malaise. An "archaeology"[2] of the American cinema is in order not because everyday life and filmic art mirror one another, nor even because some sociologists of knowledge claim that there is always some specific institutional base for every artistic expression. Rather, cinematic art—and cinematic *kitsch* as well—provide us with a mythic, and sometimes a mythopoetic picture of our collective cultural and personal dreamworlds. Despite their avarice, the commercial—and occasionally political—interests that influence the moving pictures industry act by a kind of blind cunning to present the American human condition as if it is a series of daydreams—or, often enough, nightmares.[3] The American malaise that Woody Allen captures in *Annie Hall* and *Manhattan* is a developing thing. It may be studied by an excavation of filmic theme that reveals its uneven, and occasionally self-contradictory evolution.

If we examine the relationships between men and women in American films over four decades we shall discover an extraordinary fissure threatening the very foundation of American community life. That crack, however, never quite succeeds in breaking apart the social fabric that is America. Ever broader, it engulfs more *of* our lives and more *in* our lives. Eventually it becomes a great gulf that defines as well as defies our very existence.

### The Female Principle: Ariadne

One response to anhedonic malaise—flight from America, work and, more significantly, marriage—finds expression in the subtext of war, recovery, and adventure films. In such dramas, *denouement* occurs when the male hero gives up his free and roistering life and goes off to war, promising to abjure hedonism, and to accept the responsibilities of marriage and work for the benefit of his family—once victory has been achieved. In such films heroic women—sometimes appearing as "popcorn venuses"[4] or experiencing male responses that vary from reverence to rape[5]—are armored with Ariadne's purpose: Women chasten misanthropic men, repair their social, psychic, and self-or-war-inflicted wounds, and wind them back to the world of everyday American reality—that world of competitive coexistence, compulsive conformity and driving incentives to success. Women accomplish this by employing the compelling power of their love and by counting on the pressures to heterosexuality that will eventually undermine all-male camaraderie or subvert the latent homoerotic relationship that binds the hero to his buddy. Men, or at least the heroes and their fraternity of inseparable friends, at first resist these heroines, point to their dangerous, even magical, powers, and seek escape into what soon become arenas of unfulfilling action. But ultimately they succumb to the womanly siren song. In the cinematic happy ending these heroes accept a two-step approach to their social redemption: first, courageous efforts of patriotic endeavor; second, marriage and its entailed social responsibilities.

## War and Women

Films made during World War II adjusted this theme to patriotic exigencies, presenting women not as a force compelling dyadic withdrawal,[6] blissful romance, or immediate male domestication, but rather as secret agents of national purpose, propelling men into combat.[7] In such films the male hero is all too often introduced as a disillusioned misanthrope whose past is shrouded in mystery. A woman's or his country's faithlessness is later revealed as the principal cause for his current cynicism. The war effort, to which the hero is finally restored, is but a penultimate end. Beyond it is the promise of marriage, home and family in a country that will be only seemingly different at war's end. As their foxhole conversations reveal, men in khaki look forward to becoming upwardly mobile competitors in blue collar shirts or gray flannel suits when the war is over. Family and home, however, are held out as the one secure haven in this otherwise heartless world.

Films depicting the homecoming soldier present a double-sided image of workaday routine and domesticity in postwar America. The returned veteran, sometimes physically unscathed by the war, sometimes blinded, maimed, or paralyzed as, respectively, in *Pride of the Marines* (1946), *The Best Years of Our Lives* (1946), or *Coming Home* (1978), is at first unable or unwilling to work or to effect the marriage-home-family dream that gave him incentive while he was in combat. Whatever his physical condition, his emotional state will not permit a ready and reasonable adjustment to the ordinary routines of postwar life. His "girl," however, is sympathetic and accepting. She refuses to take as final his many rebukes and insults and his warnings to get out of his life and leave him alone. Indeed, it is precisely his apparent desire for solitariness that she—and the audience—will not accept. The postwar heroine is no Ophelia so shaken by the strange demeanor and startling misogyny of her Hamlet that she goes mad and drowns herself.[8] Quite the contrary. It is she who is endlessly patient, always understanding, but firm in her love; and ultimately it is just this benéficient attitude that pays off. The hero at last admits his love, succumbs to the requirements of family life, and assumes the obligation to support it. New vistas of opportunity appear to open up for him just as he accepts her love in exchange for giving up his solitary, insecure, and self-absorbed freedom.[9]

The heroic women of wartime movies have sublimated personal needs and suppressed the anxieties of their interior lives. They are either selfless war crusaders; (Loretta Young [*China*, 1943] is an American schoolteacher shepherding a group of Chinese girls to a university where they—and, perhaps, she too—will participate in "the destiny of China;" Laraine Day [*Mr. Lucky*, 1943] is active in a home-front charitable agency, War Relief, Inc.); or they are married to active agents in the cause [Ilse, (Ingrid Bergman) is the wife of the resistance leader Victor Lazslo (Paul Henried) in *Casablanca*, 1944]. Nor do they foresee any "anhedonic" consequences for themselves or for their men arising out of their participation in the war effort. Indeed, these women conduct themselves as subtle, seductive subversives of men's liberty—and sometimes of their lives as well. But these are "good" women, justified in their patriotic cunning because we, the audience, share with them the belief that a just war obliges every able-bodied man to do his duty, and the admonition that a man's quest for irresponsible liberty is immature and illusory.

In the wartime films women have a moral and patriotic duty to send men off to war and, when the war is over, to bring them "back home." However, there is a fateful difference—and a profound danger for women and for society—between the incentive needed to push men into battle and the enticement needed to pull them home afterwards. For the first, there is the need to restore a lost self-confidence or to rekindle a flagging love of country; for the second there is the necessity to extinguish the fire of masculine independence or put out the flame of freedom from women and family responsibility that the war has lit up. Hence war movies, telling over and over of the woman's duty to send her sons and lovers off to war, must be seen against postwar films, where the limits of female patriotic endeavor are made clear. Of course in some wartime films—*China, Passage to Marseilles* (1944), *The Imposter* (1944)—the male hero's restored patriotism is but a prelude to his death; in others—e.g., *To Have and Have Not*—peacetime readjustment is mooted as hero and heroine go off on a reckless, love-as-well-as-patriotically-inspired but suicidal mission. Worthy of more extensive discussion is the ambiguous conclusion— exemplified in *Casablanca*—wherein the patriotic gesture is combined with a reassertion of male solidarity and the ever-exciting wanderlust that rejects domesticity: Rick (Humphrey Bogart) goes off to an uncertain future in the war zone near Brazzaville, arm-in-arm with Captain Renault (Claude Rains), while Ilse, who has restored Rick's confidence in himself and his country, departs for America with her resistance-leader husband. The postwar lives of the parted lovers are obscured, partly because we already know that some mysterious but never-revealed crime makes it impossible for Rick to return to America. As the film ends, we know he will join the fight in the name of the love that—having been restored to him—he has chosen magnanimously and magnificently to give up. His "final gesture," as Barbara Deming reminds us, " . . . wavers between the suicidal and the rather bleakly stoical."[10] In all such movies, the war dominates the film, and wartime is made to stand still. It is only after the war and in response to the homecoming soldier that we are permitted to see the implications that patriotism posed for those men who survived as well as those women who have waited to receive them.

Implicit in these war films is the idea that patriotic fervor is a morally correct but only *temporary* thing, "for the duration" but not beyond. But to encourage bored, disillusioned, and cynical men to become personally and ideologically attuned to the war, and to give them the incentive to march excitedly off to fight are ultimately dangerous to family and society.[11] It is not that the men might get killed or horribly wounded—certainly all of this is made clear enough in the war films—but rather that they might refuse to come back to ordinary life after they have tasted the thrilling adventure, the freedom from impersonal careerism, the all male camaraderie, or the unspeakable horrors that are parts of the battle scene.[12] Indeed, in some postwar films, it seems to be argued that the war and its female supporters on the homefront had inadvertently rekindled a primitive, immature, but powerful wanderlust in men, a wish to be free from both entangling alliances with women and the social compact.

## Homecoming and Home-making

In the postwar period, with its needs to restore economy, society, and family to antebellum orderliness, it again falls to women to act as agents of national, cultural, and socio-economic purpose. For women to participate as required, however, they must acquiesce to those revived norms of postwar society that relegate them to subordinate roles and second class citizens. Although these norms were shelved when women went to work in men's jobs during the war, they became decisive for postwar recovery. The postwar films argue that these norms provide new opportunities for women. If they will only choose to exploit their benevolent influence over men they will not only achieve personal fulfillment and supreme happiness, but also uxoricentric authority. Hence, for women, power resides in the strategic employment of sexual attractiveness, hidden behind the romantic shibboleth of the American ethic of love: A woman will bring the reluctant man around—plant trees in his blood, as Clark Gable describes Greer Garson's mysterious power over him in *Adventure* (1945)—and in the process insure that both the economic and familial institutions survive intact. For women to succeed, these films seem to state, they must give up the trappings of social and economic independence and put on a masquerade of weakness and ignorance. Films that argue this theme present at one and the same time women who *need* love in order to be fulfilled, but who will *use* love to insure that society in general, and their family in particular, get competent and responsible male support.

Stated as a moral sanction, this theme pervades all those late forties-early fifties films that present women in such occupations as corporate presidents, lawyers, doctors, or psychiatrists. These women appear to be the epitome of female independence and woman's liberation, but soon reveal themselves as loveless and lovesick and also as truly unable to manipulate men to behave in socially acceptable ways. Only when the woman comes to cherish her role as a person to be loved, to give comfort to and receive sexual favors from a deserving man does she find true happiness. Doris Day epitomized this argument in *I'll See You in My Dreams* (1955), when, as a song-writer in her own right, she meets and falls in love with Gus Kahn (Danny Thomas), gives up her career to marry him, and, as a dutiful housewife, frees him to work with better song-writers than herself. Such women also succeed in actually exercising indirect control over their men. *Spellbound* (1945), Alfred Hitchcock's thriller about a female psychiatrist's struggle to free a man from the chains of pathological self-delusion, provides a fine example.[13] Ingrid Bergman's outwardly cold medical manner—the archetypical "male" image of the female movie scientist (her patients call her "Miss Frozen Puss")—is by itself unable to relieve Gregory Peck of his affliction. But, against the advice of her own mentor (Michael Chekhov), an aged and benevolent father figure who supports her professional aspirations, she deepens her involvement, and, indeed, falls in love with her troubled patient. Peck literally runs away from her, and it appears at times that he is as frightened of her all-encompassing emotional attachment to him as he is of his own nightmarish neurosis. Bergman, however, pursues him and ultimately cures his troubled soul, exorcising the false and demonic childhood memory that has been punishing him and overcoming his reluctance to get deeply involved with a woman or a career. At the conclusion, they are married, and we are to understand that Peck will once more take up the life of an ordinary professional man, now with a good and loving wife and a promising future.

## The Career Woman as Neurotic

Women who refused to accept the manifest happiness and latent authority provided them by wifeliness, motherhood, the matrifocal household, and their moral support of family and economy, would most probably lead altogether miserable lives as independent careerists. Perhaps the single strongest representation of this theme was presented in *Sunset Boulevard* (1950), a film that parodied the death of the corrosive Hollywood star system by presenting as its protagonist Norma Desmond (Gloria Swanson), an aging and faded silent screen star, whose single-minded careerism has led her to a psychotic exploitation of those men who might have given her true happiness through marriage. Steeped in pathology, Miss Desmond insists on holding a funeral for her dead housepet, a monkey, cruelly abuses her ever-faithful ex-husband and sometime director, who now serves as her loyal and protective chauffeur (Erich von Stroheim), and murders a perceptive, if overly-ambitious gigolo (William Holden). Her insistent devotion to a career has led her to maniacal homicide.

In the postwar era, such actresses as Joan Crawford, Olivia de Haviland, Rosalind Russell, Ginger Rogers, and in a special manner to be discussed below, Eve Arden, portrayed professional career-oriented women, and were depicted as less than women, as willful or pathological opponents of the revived cultural imperative that a man should be both husband and provider. Career women are presented as persons who could achieve happiness if only they would relinquish their occupational ambitions, renounce masculine mannerisms, and give up unfulfilling independence. In some films—notably *Mildred Pierce* (1945)—the eponymous heroine's (Joan Crawford) independence is presented as but the outward sign of an internal flaw, a latent, incestuous lesbianism that expresses itself in her unrelenting shower of material benefits on an undeserving daughter (Ann Blyth). It is Mildred's pathology that generates her independence, her obsessive careerism, her rejection of her kindly and patient first husband (Bruce Bennett), and that leads to her inability to satisfy the needs of her lover, a scheming, villainous adulterer (Zachary Scott). Women who voluntarily choose a life of satisfying work when they might settle down and marry are sometimes depicted as suffering because of their perceived departure from normality. In *Take a Letter, Darling*, Rosalind Russell has in fact become the executive director of the firm in which she is a partner, while the titular head, Robert Benchley, is happily "retired," practicing golf on the office rug. Although Benchley is supportive, he exploits the substance of Russell's efforts while retaining the symbols and perquisites of his own authority. Noticing that she is having troubles, he explains that her male colleagues cannot overcome the anomaly between her gender and her occupational status:

Benchley: They don't know the difference between a woman and a. . . .
Russell: A what?
Benchley: I don't know. There's no name for you.[14]

No matter how successful or how independent, these films argue, a woman cannot be truly happy, cannot achieve a wholesome female existence, without a man, love, marriage, and family. In *Lady in the Dark*, Ginger Rogers portrays a successful fashion editor whose "suits and strident manner . . . signaled her difference from other women and her lack of all those things—love, sex, husband-master—that make a woman happy."[15] And it is in this film that a woman's aspiration for an independent career is professionally diagnosed as a symptom of mental illness. Troubled by nightmares that psychotherapy ultimately reveals to be the aftereffects of an unhappy childhood, Rogers seeks help from a male analyst who redefines her careerism as an unhealthy compensatory device:

> Psychoanalyst: You've had to prove you were superior to
> all men; you had to dominate them.
> Rogers: What's the answer?
> Psychoanalyst: Perhaps some man who'll dominate you.[16]

Femininity, an outward sign of internal sex-role adjustment, has been sacrificed by those women who seek careers in business or in the professions. Even when presented as such heroines as Bette Davis' librarian who resists book censorship (*Storm Center*, 1956), spinster professionals are invariably dressed as Victorian old maids. Katharine Hepburn has essayed many such roles since she played Sydney Fairfield, a woman who decides to give up romance and marriage to take care of her mad father (John Barrymore) in *A Bill of Divorcement* (1932). In *The African Queen* (1951) she appears as a strong-willed spinster, sister to a missionary, who is rescued from spending her life as a lonely old maid by the love of a raffish riverboat captain (Humphrey Bogart); four years later Miss Hepburn sealed the fate of the tragic spinster in her moving portrayal of an unmarried schoolteacher who loses her one chance for self-fulfilling love by refusing the ministrations of a kindly Italian businessman (Rossano Brazzi) who, although bound by an unbreakable marriage, would gladly make Hepburn his mistress (*Summertime*, 1955). When women portray doctors or psychiatrists (Claudette Colbert in *Private Worlds*, Ingrid Bergman in *Spellbound*) their characters, as Molly Haskell has noticed, are "drawn as brisk and efficient, with the implication that they arrived at their level of competence only by suppressing their female natures."[17] Women in business are even more mannish and less feminine in their dress and deportment. Hence the decision to attire Joan Crawford, Ginger Rogers, and Eve Arden in sharply defined masculine suits with heavy shoulder pads whenever they portrayed career-seekers.

Eve Arden presents a special instance of this theme. Her multi-faceted characterization of the female "buddy" who provides moral support for the businesswoman heroine evokes the clearest delineation of the losses for femininity entailed in choosing career over marriage, family, and childrearing. On the surface Arden (in *Mildred Pierce*) seems to be the perfect friend for the aspiring career-woman. Witty and wise, she appears so well adjusted to the requirements of job and career—spinsterhood and a rough and ready toughness of mind—that she might serve as an advertisement for women's liberation. A closer look, however, suggests that her incessant barrage of withering wisecracks and her ever-ready ripostes hide a deep emotional scar, a repressed self-hatred and unconscious feelings of inferiority about her failures as a woman. Molly Haskell observes that, "She is made to talk constantly and longingly of men, to deprecate her own powers of attraction, to place greater emphasis on sex than all the silly ninny sex objects who have nothing else to live for, in short, constantly to bemoan her 'incompleteness'."[18] Arden portrayed the business and professional woman's best friend so well that she went on to develop the role into a career and a stereotype. As "Our Miss Brooks," a radio (1948-1951), film (1955), and television character (1952-1955), Arden came to personify the modern American spinster schoolteacher. Intelligent and with a gentle self-deprecating sense of humor, "Miss Brooks" guides her doting male students who sometimes develop adolescent crushes on her, into secure job-directed studies and her female students toward marriage and motherhood, but she firmly fends off the romantic marriage-mindedness of her endlessly patient and mildly effete male-teacher suitor. Precisely because she is outspoken and clever about matters of sex and about men in general, Arden's woman is never a salable commodity on the marriage market. Her brains and charm, and her genuine but hidden longing for a man, are all made to work against her own marital happiness. She serves in the end as a symbol and a warning to other women: aggressive self-assertion and determination to succeed in a man's portion of the world will inexorably lead to loveless loneliness. Here is the horror of the half-known life, assuaged only in part by friendships with other women similarly situated.

Films of the fifties, Marjorie Rosen has observed, repressed women; they "precluded [their] exploration of life, squelched [their] fantasies, and inhibited [their] sexuality."[19] If the repressed masculine Eve Ardens priced themselves out of the marriage market by being too masculine and seeming to know too much about men, men's work, and sex, the horror fantasies of the decade suggested that female sexual aggressiveness threatened both man and society. Such an orientation was presented in the *She Creature* (1956), wherein a voluptuous woman becomes so powerful that she literally threatens mankind itself. Fantasizing women as fiends— e.g., the Ape Woman (Aquanetta in the 1943 production, *Captive Wild Woman*), the Snake Woman (Jacqueline Pearce in *The Reptile*, 1966), the *Wasp Woman* (1959), or the *Leech Woman* (1960), (the latter two were ordinary women transformed into female monsters by the application of super-potent cosmetics or chemical formulae designed to perpetuate youth)—these films spoke to the terrors inspired by unrepressed female sexuality and implicitly argued in behalf of the shy, coy, and demure lady who proved virginal until marriage and faithful ever after.[20] Even before the fifties' fantasies, realistic films presented evil women as employing excessive zeal in acquiring material possessions (Rosalind Russell as *Craig's Wife* [1936]), or as callously rejecting the shabby hut she lives in (a "dump"), turning against her effete husband and children and wanting to run off to the high life of Chicago (Bette Davis in *Beyond the Forest* [1949]). The good woman, then, had to steer a careful course. She had to need love and want to give and receive it. She had to look rapturously toward becoming a mother (Dorothy McGuire painfully learns to behave like both a proper wife and a mother, to let go of her mother's apron strings, to take charge of her home, and to assume responsibility for her baby, in the two-film series *Claudia* [1943] and *Claudia and David* [1946]). She should encourage her husband to become a sober, determined and eager breadwinner, but not to become so aggressive in his career-seeking that he loses sight of the law, propriety, or the warmth of hearth and home. In *Double Indemnity* (1944) Barbara Stanwyck epitomizes the evil woman because she is not only a conniving homewrecker but also a seductress who lures Fred MacMurray away from honest employment and into committing fraud, larceny, and murder. If she works, it should be to help out not supplant her husband, and she should take care not to emasculate her man by indicating a more than temporary or casual interest in her own occupation or ability to manage her life. When Milly Stephenson

(Myrna Loy), in *The Best Years of Our Lives*, tells her returned soldier husband (Fredric March) how much she enjoys being both breadwinner and homemaker and daughter Peggy (Teresa Wright) adds, "You don't have to worry about us, Dad. We can handle the problems," the unhappy veteran complains to Derry (Dana Andrews), his wartime comrade, that coming home "feels like I were going in to hit a beach." Even if she should be a naive nymphet, unworldly and uneducated, and seem to be interested only in a teasing but virginal round of fun with the beach boys, the true woman should be morally committed not only to a love-based marriage but also to a solid and secure man freed from any brooding disillusion or anguished cynicism: In *Gidget* (1959), Sandra Dee's mother explains that the family slogan is "To be a real woman is to bring out the best in a man," and Gidget proves herself a real chip off her mother's block as, young, pigtailed, nubile, and very vulnerable, she nevertheless guides her somewhat older boyfriend (Cliff Robertson) away from an aimless life of surfing and back to his former profession as a pilot. Moreover, films of the fifties also argued that marriage and family were the sure sources of happiness for men and women of the working class as well. In *Marty* (1954) a plain and ordinary, rotund butcher (Ernest Borgnine) finds and gives happiness to a spinster schoolteacher (Betsy Blair), who thought she was too many years beyond the marrying age and doomed to a loveless life.

## Liberty and the Male Principle

On the surface marriage, family, and a good job or promising career are presented as both achievable and desirable goals for most Americans in that period. Yet underneath their manifest argument, these films suggest quite the opposite. If good women benefit from a compassionate marriage and bask in the reflected status of their husband's occupation, good men are pictured as their grudgingly acquiescent victims. The world of regular work is all too often presented as a pitiless destroyer of male elan, grinding down masculine individuality and converting the working man into a mere cog in the giant industrial or corporate machine. Hence, these women are dangerous because they demand more than a good time, will take nothing less than marriage, and hold

out for the security of the routinized life. At bottom the heroes
of these films suspect that the promises of the good life symbolized
by a happy marriage and a good job are false. Barbara Deming
has analyzed the plots of seven films released in 1945 and 1946—
*Love Letters, State Fair, Those Endearing Young Charms,
Adventure, Lost Weekend, Spellbound,* and *Pride of the Marines*—
and shown that despite considerable differences in settings, style,
and genre, each of these stories tells of the hero's vain resistance
to what he believes is a vague but powerful institutionalization
of bad faith.[21] In each film, however, the male hero is led to
reconceive his apprehensions as a pathology rooted in unconscious
fears about his own masculinity. In *Those Endearing Young
Charms,* Laraine Day tells Robert Young, "You're afraid of yourself,
not of me," when he resists her attempts to make more out of his
love-making than he wants; in *Adventure* Greer Garson imagines
Clark Gable to be "like an animal caught in a trap or a maze!
You try to help him and he turns on you, afraid you'll tear his
heart out!" In *State Fair* Dana Andrews tells Jeanne Crain, "If
I really cared for a girl, I'd care too much to wish a guy like me
off on her!" And in *Love Letters,* Joseph Cotten bemoans the fact
that Jennifer Jones is "in love with my letters—a man who doesn't
exist!" In *Pride of the Marines, Lost Weekend,* and *Spellbound*
the hero is clearly troubled by self-doubts that arise from a
diagnosed infirmity—blindness, alcoholism, and amnesia,
respectively—but each of these is made out to be a pathetic and
ultimately unacceptable excuse for his unconscious doubts about
whether he can measure up to what American society expects of
a normal man. In each of these films the woman ultimately
triumphs over the man's self-doubt. Not only does she convince
him that his fears are groundless or, worse, evidence of immature
cowardice, she also persuades him to accept as a worthy truth
what he has always suspected is a dishonorable lie and a clever
fraud—that it is not bad faith to become part of conformist
workaday American society, to aspire to be a man who wants
nothing more than a warm and loving home, a supportive
companion-wife, and a steady job.

More openly in the 1930s but less obviously in the 1950s,
American films suggest that the true traits of masculinity are
expressed, forged, and tested in situations of solitary wandering,
in war or police work, as a pioneer or trail-blazer, or in the company
of other men equally dedicated to the male life. From this point
of view, women occupy an ambiguous place in a man's life. They

need defense, deserve respect, give comfort—but they expect marriage. Thus, women are necessary for a man's ego and sexual demands, but insufficient to satisfy his basic needs. More to the point, the good woman, precisely because she demands marriage, threatens to destroy once and for all men's basic source of masculinity—the free, roving, irresponsible life. The battle between the sexes is also, then, a struggle within each of them over which principle—the free masculine or the fettered feminine—will triumph and how it will do so.

In literally hundreds of films heroic men stand, or desire to stand, outside of society. Society and the settled life hold out little attraction to these men; indeed, towns and cities and the habits and routines that daily life in them encourages sometimes frighten these men far more than the bandits, spies, enemy troops, or giant beasts that they must overcome in order to survive. These heroes appear as *wanderers*—seamen, frontiersmen, soldiers of fortune, self-displaced foreigners; as *adventurers*—private detectives, migratory cowboys, hunters, mercenaries, espionage agents; as *marginal men*—deracinated emigrants from culture, lumpenprole-tarians without permanent or promising employment, beach-combers, life-guards, or surfers. So long as the world presented itself as incompletely discovered, not yet fully explored, only partially settled, or subject to revolution and war, these men could be portrayed as agents of imperial advance, pioneers of frontier settlement, less than filial sons, or disillusioned lovers. Typically these men flee parents, friends, women, and responsibility and enter into troubled areas, or they are devil-may-care youths who rush off to war and adventure without any sense of the dangers involved. It is no wonder that cinema historian Kevin Brownlow discovers that the first reel-life exciting films, where men could be men, were plotted or documented around the war, the west, and the wilderness, and filmed away from Hollywood in distant and dangerous places.[22] Even when land frontiers seemed no longer available, filmmakers could place solitary, heroic men in the air, on uninhabited planets, or under the sea, that is, beyond the pale of civilization and free of women, matrimony, and social convention.

Women threaten men's freedom not only because they tie them down with marriage but also because they are the special agents of civilization and all its attendant conventions, institutions, and discontents. In the films it is women who even in time of war support the long view that education will save the future generations (Loretta Young in *China*); are committed to piety and church-going (in countless westerns, but memorably in *High Noon*

[1952], when Amy Kane's [Grace Kelly] Quakerism acts as a temporary hindrance to her husband Will's [Gary Cooper] single-handed defense of the town); foster prudent intellectualism (in *Adventure* librarian Emily Sears [Greer Garson] offers the anxious Harry [Clark Gable] and his deeply-troubled seafaring pal, Mudgin [Thomas Mitchell], a philosophy book when they seek relief and refuge from their nameless fears); and place the family uppermost in their hierarchy of values. (In *Random Harvest* [1942] Paula [Greer Garson] waits patiently for nearly two decades, in the interim aiding her amnesiac husband's [Ronald Colman] business and political career until he recovers his memory, remembers that she is his wife, and comes home to their vine-covered cottage in the country.) It is precisely these aspects and trappings of civilization, with their effete overblown pretensions, excessively moralistic pieties, and obligatory responsibilities that men suspect will restrict their liberties and routinize and deaden their lives. As Stanley Cavell puts it, "When the man goes home to his wife, his life is over."[23]

In the Western film, the hero opposes the arbitrary strength of other strong men, but even more forcefully he resists the restless discontent that would be imposed on him if he accepted the constraints of civilization for which he fights. Freud points out that the essence of civilization—the content of that form wherein the personal liberty of the individual is restrained by the social power of the community—"lies in the fact that the members of the community restrict themselves in their possibilities of satisfaction, whereas the individual knew no such restrictions."[24] For the Western community, satisfaction is limited to the domesticated happiness and social security that law, order, and—most significantly—family and family responsibilities will insure. The hero refuses or rebels against this form of partial happiness for himself at the same time that he selflessly fights to protect it for others. In the older, classical form of the genre, he rides away in the last reel, leaving behind a love-lorn girlfriend and a grateful township, reasserting his special place outside of society and free of its social and matrimonial controls. The classical Western poses quite directly society's dilemma—the search for the appropriate balance between individual freedom and social security. Good, homeloving women in such films represent a one-sided resolution of that problem. Men, they seem to argue, should be willing to give up their claim to personal liberty in exchange for a woman's faithful love and the warmth and security that home and settled existence provide.

The films of the 30s, 40s and 50s held with varying degree of intensity and considerable ambiguity that marriage and settling down were the proper forms within which civilization would accommodate a restricted range of human liberty. In so doing, however, these films pitted men against women; for the former, freedom and personal fulfillment are fundamental desires obtained by refusing matrimonial ties and resisting comfortable domesticity; for the latter, happiness and security are basic ideals, whose accomplishment is signalled by catching and holding onto a male partner. Women subtly courted or brassily chased after men; men were flattered by the attention but opposed to the objective. Both sexes were caught up in the struggle that made them lovers and enemies simultaneously. Perhaps no genre gave greater play to the agonizing ambiguities of this paradox than the Western. In the classical Western, male heroes are typically loners without sweethearts, wives, families, or permanent ties to any community, and without any desire to acquire them.[25] Speaking of the hero's self-imposed social isolation, Stanley J. Solomon suggests that "apparently the ultimate motive for this persistent quality stems from the deepest aspect of the character's nature, which, as far as I know, has never been described by any character in the genre."[26] The hero senses that he doesn't belong, that he won't fit in, that he would be frustrated by any kind of permanent entangling alliance. In *Pursued* (1947), Robert Mitchum portrays a cowboy who is deeply troubled by self-doubts, arising from the fact that he is an adopted child—i.e., he comes from nowhere and he has nowhere to go, but he is constantly pursued by those who would give him a meaningful place in society. At the same time the hero is a reformer and, sometimes, a rebel, but never a revolutionary. His stand against cattle thieves, claim jumpers, crooked sheriffs, and cutthroats serves to protect and bolster the community and the domestic life which he ultimately rejects or, in post-classical Westerns, before which he ultimately succumbs. His resistance to marriage and a permanent home are to be taken not as a moral or social indictment of these institutions but rather as a personal statement. The hero admires and is attracted to marriage and community life, but unwilling to surrender his freedom in order to enjoy their blessings.

One source of the hero's ambivalence is the character of the woman in Western films. To be sure the "unsullied pioneer heroine" and the "saloon girl" are archetypical figures in Westerns,[27] but over the years the former, as Fenin and Everson have shown,[28] has been outfitted with a stronger character that increasingly challenges and frightens men. At first pioneer wives and sweethearts were endowed with perseverance and grit; later, they deteriorated into frail and dependent creatures, requiring more loving care and tender solicitation than the hero cared to give; and still later they acquired a new, more sexual self-reliance and a sensual appeal that was hidden beneath their outwardly Victorian sensibilities. Even more than the earlier heroines, the later, more complex versions of western women tend to mystify and frighten heroic men and confuse them over which path to choose—freedom and gnawing isolation, or romantic marriage and dreary discontent.

That men are hopelessly caught up in the painful choice between a free but lonesome life outside of society or a promising but unattractive matrimonial and career existence within it is dramatically illustrated in King Vidor's film, *Duel in the Sun* (1946). Although its background is the epic conflict between Senator McCanles (Lionel Barrymore), a pioneer patriarch who has opened the West, and the nameless, faceless corporate bodies that would eventually civilize it, the central theme is the fateful love triangle affecting the McCanles sons. Lewt (Gregory Peck) and Jesse (Joseph Cotten), compete for the body and soul of Pearl Chavez (Jennifer Jones). The general dilemma of men in American society is decomposed monodramatically[29] into the characters of these two brothers, Lewt, the lewd, lusty, loner, and Jesse, the sophisticated, Victorian gentleman. And the female mystique is similarly divided into the polished, faithful, homemaker wife, Helen (Joan Tetzel), and the wild, sensuous, uncivilized seductress, Pearl. Symbolizing the fatal combination that arises when civilization is compromised with savagery, Pearl the untamed and doomed beauty, is presented as a half-breed, the daughter of a drunken bohemian (Herbert Marshall) and an exotic, voluptuous Indian princess (Tilly Losch). The subtext of the film is that man's search for solitary freedom is but a death wish, and that civilization, propriety, wife, family, and deadening routine are all that one should expect—or settle for—out of life. Lewt, Gregory Peck's cinematic character essay in confused libertinism, is too much the free spirit to ever accept marriage ("no woman is going to tie onto me," he tells Pearl, "least of all a little half-breed like you.") and too desirous of exclusive possession to let Pearl marry someone else and become civilized. He shoots Sam Pierce (Charles Bickford), the middle-aged man who has become engaged to her, and, when Jesse offers Pearl a home and the opportunity to become a proper lady like his own wife ("She's a lady, ain't she?" Pearl asks. "Like you're going to be," Jesse assures her), Lewt challenges Pearl to come to him at Squaw's Head rock for what will be a murderous *Liebestod*.

But Jesse's motives are also ambivalent and confused. After witnessing Lewt's rape of Pearl—a scene out of his own repressed desires—Jesse retreats to the safer but sensually unchallenging arms of Helen, a polite and civilized woman of his own race, class, and color. Nevertheless, he is still drawn helplessly to Pearl: When he leaves her and the ranch to establish an honest reputation and prove that he can be self-made with both an independent career and a respectable wife, Jesse confesses to Pearl that "I loved you . . . Somehow you touched me . . . I was going to come back for you someday." Unable to leave off of her even after he marries Helen, Jesse asks her to come and live with him and his wife and let them remold her into a refined, unsensual woman, fit for marriage and polite society. Like his alter-ego, Lewt, Jesse cannot stand to be with or without Pearl, the female symbol of untamable lust and the heart of darkness to which he is attracted but cannot entrust himself. His benevolent attempt to civilize her is but the projection of his wish to kill that aspect of Lewt that is still buried inside of himself, his own unconscious desire to escape from the confines of civil society and matrimonial respectability. When Pearl and Lewt duel to their deaths in the pitiless sun, they at one and the same time apotheosize and sacrifice the Dionysian pleasure that can never be experienced by those who acquiesce to civilization and respectability.

## Moral Man in Absurd Society

If the Western lends ambiguous moral support to community and marriage, its modern counterpart, the gangster-crime-detective story, threatens matrimony and civilization, suggesting that behind their beneficent facades there is nothing but bad faith, corruption, and self-delusion. Examination of such films as *The Maltese Falcon* (1941) and *D.O.A.* (1949), suggests that the demoralization of Western culture begins when the hopes of love, marriage and family are dashed and men discover there is no exit from a dis-eased civilization.

Of what are called *noir* films, *The Maltese Falcon* stands out
for its presentation of corruptible men and women in corrupt
society. Nothing is sacred in this grey drama of thievery,
conspiracy, faithlessness, and dishonor. Sam Spade (Humphrey
Bogart), a private detective, takes over the case of Miss Wundalay
(Mary Astor) after his partner Miles Archer (Jerome Cowan) is
mysteriously gunned down on the first night of the investigation.
Everything about Miss Wundalay's story is deceptive or false, even
her name. Eventually, her sophisticated veneer is removed, and
she is revealed as Brigid O'Shaughnessy, a scheming and
murderous temptress who will stop at nothing to get possession
of the supremely valuable Maltese falcon, a jewel-encrusted statue.
Her partners and competitors in this deadly quest are Kasper
Gutman (Sydney Greenstreet), a corpulent confidence man, whose
European polish and exquisite tastes in liquor and clothing barely
cover his shabby and amoral interests in acquiring wealth and
power, and Joel Cairo (Peter Lorre), a perfumed and gloved
Continental homosexual, whose effete ways convey a bitchy black
comedy of criminal errors.

Society, in *The Maltese Falcon*, is inherently corrupt, yet there
is no way around or out of it. All humans are after money, power,
and status, and they employ brute strength or brittle cunning to
get them. To be moral in this immoral society, one has to hide
one's ethical light under a bushel of cynical self-interest and run
the risk of being corrupted by one's own amoral masquerade. Such
is the case with Sam Spade. Spade is at first cynically amused
by Miss Wundalay's deceiving ways, but gradually, reluctantly,
indeed, against his better nature which at the end reasserts itself
in an effort of ethical will, he is drawn to this conniving seductress.
The corrosive society finds its quintessential counterpart in this
woman who, as Spade's final scene with her cruelly reveals, cannot
be reformed by love. Man deserves his achingly-desired aloneness
and the right to be free from this corrupting influence, but, this
film argues, he cannot escape from the desperation that freedom
entails.

Women no longer possess those homemaking qualities of love
and companionship. This is not only the case with Brigid
O'Shaughnessy, but also with all the other women in *The Maltese
Falcon*. Ivy Archer (Gladys George) is a promiscuous bitch, whose
interest in the high life and a round of male escorts and bedmates,
has only temporarily settled on Spade, her late husband's partner
and her secret paramour during the marriage. Even the patient

and loyal Effie Perine (Lee Patrick) is less than sensible in her judgments (she believes Miss O'Shaughnessy's story, and tells Spade to trust her) and when Spade compliments her, it is for her "masculine" courage and her ability to take things like a man. Moreover, this film contains one identified homosexual (Joel Cairo) and two men whose sexual preferences are ambiguous but potentially oriented toward those of their own sex (Kasper Gutman and Wilmer Cook [Elisha Cook, Jr.]). These less-than-men, representatives in various oblique ways of the amoral female principle in society, are also vicious and venal, absolutely untrustworthy, and warning icons of what an ethical man must avoid or overcome if he is to survive. At the end, when Spade has finally sorted out all the sordid details of the labyrinthine mystery, discovered that all the protagonists are enmeshed in crime, and proven to his own almost masochistic satisfaction that Miss O'Shaughnessy is indeed the murderess he had suspected her to be, he resists her piteous pleas for his love and sympathy. "I won't play the sap for you," Spade replies, and, as Barbara Deming has observed, what he means by this is not only that he won't go to prison for her, but, even more significantly, "that he intends to remain a free agent."[30] At the end of *The Maltese Falcon* Spade sends Miss O'Shaughnessy off to jail with two detectives aboard an elevator, whose short vertical journey to the street symbolizes the decreased span of direction that urban life has imposed on man's freedom. Although still a free agent, Sam Spade can only follow Miss O'Shaughnessy and the police down to the street, into the city, and toward that isolated loneliness that must take the place of individual freedom in the contemporary world.

Perhaps the darkest version of the male illusion of the female's freedom and the female's of domestic security is contained in Rudolph Mate's 1949 film, *D.O.A.*. To even seek escape from the American routine of doting love, dull job, and dreary existence is presented as a self-deluding, black comedy of death. As the film opens we learn that the hero is about to die, and he wants to tell a skeptical police department about why he is dying and who killed him. Accountant Frank Bigelow (Edmond O'Brien), a quintessentially ordinary man, lives in Banning, a hot, stifling small town, fretfully engaged to the faithful but smothering Paula (Pamela Britton). Attempting to get away for a time, Bigelow takes a trip to San Francisco, a city, Joan Didion would later remind us, that is on the farthest frontier shore of America, where suicides are inordinately high, and where people fleeing from the death-in-life of middle America expect life to be better, because there is no place farther to go. If Banning is dull, San Francisco is flashy with false veneer. Bigelow is caught up in the blaring music, tawdry sensuality, and glaring lights that speak to the hopelessness into which he has escaped. On his first night in the city, he is fatally poisoned when someone slips a lethal dose of a mysterious substance for which there is no known antidote into his drink. None of this makes any sense to Bigelow, to the physicians who diagnose his sure death or to the audience watching the film. That is just the point. Bigelow has entered the urban world of meaninglessness, where nothing makes sense, no one cares about anyone, and there is nothing that anyone will do about it. *D.O.A.* is an absurdist parody of the Protestant Ethic. That ethic—inspired by Calvin's inexorable logic—had moved the Puritans to plunge into the uncertainties of worldly activity in the hope of uncovering a sign of their election in the world to come. In *D.O.A.* the dying Bigelow is moved by the awesome mystery of his plight to plunge into the crazy, corrupt, depraved, and menacing underworld in quest of whoever has poisoned him and why. However, his triumph of born again *virtu* over fatal *fortuna* is ultimately hollow.[31]

*D.O.A.* presents both the sexuality of the bad girl and the joys of wife, family and home as deceptive traps for men. Paula, the good woman, lives in a dug-out of vapid domesticity—where even the local bar offers nothing more exciting than televised horse races, a bored policeman, and a juke-box that plays out-of-date love songs—dreamily inured to the dullness of her daily life in the desert town. Bigelow has fled from this prison house of conventionalism as one would flee from death, but he finds that the spicier women of San Francisco provide neither zest nor fulfillment. Life has reached its end-point before death takes its inevitable toll. Neither the loving woman, the warm hearth, the safe and secure home that promises to be a haven, nor the adventurous life on the urban frontier with loose and sensual women who ask for nothing more than a good time will revive the *elan vital*. Bigelow must die, Jack Shadoian tells us, "because he is . . . one who wants more than what life will yield."[32] To such a man women have lost their allure: they can only offer life as it is, and that is not enough.

*From Noir to Anhedonia*

The immediate reaction to the chilling message of *noir* films was reactive denial. During the 50s, Hollywood desperately sought to resuscitate the promise of fulfillment and the good life that would come from marriage and husband's pursuit of a career. It attempted this by means of a series of wholesome comedies superficially celebrating the theme of girl-chases-half-heartedly-resistant-boy-until-he-succumbs (the Rock Hudson-Doris Day pictures that virtually represented 50s ideology).

The women in these films were lovely but chaste, charming but in need of masculine affection and support. Their moral surety insured a moral family thriving in a moral society. But, in 1958 Alfred Hitchcock released *Vertigo*, a dark thriller that dashed forever the male's wish to fashion his own perfect female companion, one who would combine the sensuality of the "bad girl" with the uncomplicated loving that a man needed in order to be secure in his freedom, free in his security. *Vertigo* showed that this desire is founded on a self-deceiving stereotype of female malleability, as well as a self-deluding exaggeration of man's power to shape people to his will. When Ferguson (James Stewart) discovers that the dowdy Judy, whom he has transformed into the delightful but supposedly dead Madeleine (Kim Novak), are one in the same person, and that he has actually been tricked into participating in a murderous conspiracy that he was hired to prevent, he is utterly lost. Betrayed by his friend and bewitched by his passion, he is left bewildered by the fateful turn of events. *Vertigo* put an end to the powerful male's dream of finding the perfect woman. It called upon all dreamers of such a *denouement* to wake up. But the wakefulness to which it invited them was fitful and restive. It evoked a pervasive anxiety but offered no release from it.

Central to the malaise that enveloped Hollywood characters in the 'sixties and after is disillusion with the family. In the older Hollywood formula, the film ended with a loving kiss that sealed the matrimonial bargain between a man and a woman who loved and deserved one another. Their subsequent life as a married couple was left to the imagination of the audience, who were led to suppose that, as in the old fairy tales, they lived happily ever after. However, if women will not accept monogamous marital companionship as a replacement for sensual romance, refuse reflected status and seek careers and public recognition in their own names, and demand every jot and tittle of equality that the law and their own individual and collective efforts might obtain, the troubles between the sexes are just beginning when the organ plays the wedding march. With *Kramer vs. Kramer* (1979) and *Ordinary People* (1980), Hollywood opened the home life of the hitherto happy family to critical inspection. The American family lacked love, companionability, nurturance, and clearcut gender responsibility. In each of these films it is important to note how a woman's liberation from a stifling marriage is won at the price of her dignity and relevance. The career-seeking Mrs. Kramer (Meryl Streep) proves herself capable of making it in the world of professionals—indeed, at the time of the divorce she is earning more than her husband—but she has deliberately chosen to desert her child, who is shown to need and respond to parental love. Although Mr. Kramer's (Dustin Hoffman) career advancement has suffered because he has had to take over his wife's domestic and nurturant responsibilities, he has proved himself to be effective as both a surrogate mother and a provider. Women might be necessary for procreation, this film suggests, but properly chastened and responsible men are sufficient for maintenance of the family. *Ordinary People* goes even further in documenting the decline of the middle class American family. The cold and heartless mother (Mary Tyler Moore) maintains a household but has deserted her domestic duties, driving her son (Timothy Hutton) to attempt suicide, while her effete and feckless husband (Donald Sutherland) is left to wring his hands in helpless despair. Only a helpful outsider, a Jewish psychiatrist (Judd Hirsch) can provide partial resolution to this family's many problems. The son is helped to stand on his own two feet and brought to recognize that his father's ineffectiveness is not entirely without character. However, the mother leaves, and we are to believe that father and son will do quite well without her. The battle between men and women might go on, these films seem to say but a newly constituted all male homestead is likely to become the long sought haven within the world, while the workplace will be the scene of competitive coexistence and a cold war of the sexes.

In the 70s and 80s Hollywood films have sought still another escape from malaise. The Western has virtually disappeared and with it cinema's most direct memorial to femininity's support of civilization. A new genre of fantasies aims at deflecting perceptions from the real world and toward a comic book society of self-mocking heroics. The old values that their heroes purport to serve are treated to tongue-in-cheek discreditation. Horror films and thrillers treat their teenage audiences to the claim that Halloween is a time of mindless and sadistic mayhem, sleepaway camps are places for illicit sex and murderous carnage, and the house on Elm Street is the residence of a child-hating monster who savages what little love and security are left in the family home. The immigrant's dream of rising to a place of honor in America has been disenchanted in the quartet of *Rocky* films: When Italian American Rocky Balboa (Sylvester Stallone) rises from Philadelphia street hood to world heavyweight champion, he finds that he is merely a celebrity to the massive lonely crowd that has replaced his old neighborhood gang. Together with his wife (Talia Shire) and her brother (Burt Young), a morose Rocky resides in a chilly and inhospitable mansion. Their only companions are a set of expensive, mechanical robots, one of whom serves as a surrogate girlfriend for "The Italian Stallion's" pathetically loveless brother-in-law. Woody Allen's comment has come full circle. The terrifying problems of the universe—civilization and its discontents—have fostered the neuroses that are *de rigeur* not only for Rocky and his family.

In retrospect, it now appears that *D.O.A.* put finis to the American dream. The security and satisfaction that once arose out of rising to the top of one's profession are revealed to be either false or illusory. Not only is Bigelow bored and enervated by his successes as an accountant, he is also murdered because of an innocent inadvertency arising out of his perfectly lawful practice. The ethical admonition to engage in hard work no longer serves to evoke a meaningful sign of election, a point made directly in the film when the utterly perplexed Bigelow looks up to the heavens for some answer to his plight and is momentarily blinded by the pitiless glare of the blank sun. Without time to enjoy any benefits from his life-long efforts in an honest pursuit, and separated forever from the admittedly unenticing embrace of his "best girl," Bigelow is without hope. His position is truly anomic. With only memories of a past to which he cannot return and bereft of any future, Bigelow is spiritually dead the moment his fatal condition is diagnosed; his physical demise in the police station merely ratifies the human condition to which his life had already brought him.

The *noir* dramas repudiate the old ideal that holds that women are loving preservers of moral society, but it does not replace it with a new one. Women are relegated to the most ignominious status of all—irrelevance.

### Conclusion

The depth of the fissure dividing the sexes became visible only after Hollywood cleared away the sentimentalism and enchantment that had covered it. That cover had helped to preserve and protect the American dream against the subversive potential of realism. The dream had been rooted in the commitment of women to the saving institutions of church, school, and family. Hollywood presented that theme most directly in the Western where religion, education, and child rearing are not only the foundations of the social order but are brought to fruition by tender-hearted but tough-minded women who overcome the heroic man's commitment to free agentry.

For a modern man to remain a free agent, he would have to risk both affection and security. A truly free life, as the movies make clear in hundreds of scenarios celebrating at the same time as they deny this American mystique, requires denial of permanent human association, giving up the love and companionship of women, and a refusal to settle down to marriage and responsibility. Hence, most of the films that speak to this theme treat the loneliness of the hero as a self-absorbed unconscious or only half-confessed longing. As Michael Wood has observed, "We long to be lonely, that is, even as we go in search of others. . . ."[33] Whereas the good woman in the Western stood for the good society that could be built and maintained with her support, and the good-bad girl, (e.g., Claire Trevor, as the prostitute in *Stagecoach* [1939])[34] showed the lonesome highwayman (John Wayne as the Ringo Kid in the same film) the way to domestication and an honest job, the women of later contemporary urban dramas are character studies in deception. Ultimately, they point up the irrelevance of their sex for assuaging the agonies that have overtaken modern man. By extension, the good society to which women demand their men pledge allegiance is also shown to be a fraud.

The war films of the 40s emphasized that national defense depended on heroines who, combining unflagging belief in the American way with self-sacrificing love of sweethearts and husbands, rekindled patriotic spirit among cynical or disillusioned men. However, the postwar economy required cinema's women to withdraw from war-related jobs, return to their prewar status as doting girlfriends and dependent wives, but subtly steer the homecoming veterans into the restorative normalcy of matrimony and civilian work. Throughout all of this, women had had to struggle against the male opposition to civilization's restrictions on hedonism, irresponsibility, and isolation. However, once the family was shown to be a hollow shell and work had lost its power to enthrall men, the dream began to fade.

With *D.O.A.*, Hollywood had revealed the dystopia toward which both the male and female variants of the American dream had been tending. Until the *noir* films, American cinema had functioned as a dream factory, keeping alive the hope that somehow American men and women would each find an appropriate measure of freedom and security in their lives. The malaise that Woody Allen would present as the inescapable tragi-comedy of the American urbanite of the 1970s and 1980s could not be completely revealed until the daydreams of both sexes had been disenchanted and reproduced as nightmares. However, revelation and disenchantment are the proper activities of secular prophets, the task usually assigned to the man of knowledge as an essential part of his social role. When Hollywood assumed this burden, it could not provide a way out nor could it offer a path to utopia. The yellow brick road, as the movie indicated, led only to the false *Wizard of Oz* (1939) a charlatan who responded to Dorothy's and her friends' needs by telling them to search for the psychic strengths already resident in their hearts and minds. The message that our own psychic self-sufficiency would have to do for each of us was not lost on the subsequent oracles of *noir* dramas; rather, it was respecified: This ingredient, so vital to modern life, was both unevenly distributed and in short supply.

## Reference Notes

1. Joan Didion, August 16, 1979, "Letter from 'Manhattan'," *New York Review of Books*, XXVI: 13: pp. 18–19.
2. The term "archaeology" is taken over in part from two works of Michel Foucalt, THE ORDER OF THINGS: AN ARCHAEOLOGY OF THE HUMAN SCIENCES, (New York: Pantheon Books, Random House, 1970), and THE ARCHAEOLOGY OF KNOWLEDGE, AND THE DISCOURSE ON LANGUAGE, trans. by A. M. Sheridan Smith (New York: Pantheon Books, Random House, 1972).
3. An excellent statement of this position is found in Barbara Deming, RUNNING AWAY FROM MYSELF: A DREAM PORTRAIT OF AMERICA DRAWN FROM THE FILMS OF THE FORTIES, (New York: Grossman Publishers, 1969).
4. See Marjorie Rosen, POPCORN VENUS: WOMEN, MOVIES, AND THE AMERICAN DREAM, (New York: Avon Books, 1973).
5. Molly Haskell, FROM REVERENCE TO RAPE: THE TREATMENT OF WOMEN IN THE MOVIES, (Baltimore: Penguin Books, 1974).
6. For the psycho-social issues involved in dyadic withdrawal see Philip Slater, "Social Limitations on Libidinal Withdrawal," *AMERICAN JOURNAL OF SOCIOLOGY*, 67, (November, 1961), pp. 296–311, and Stanford M. Lyman, THE SEVEN DEADLY SINS: SOCIETY AND EVIL, (New York: St. Martin's Press, 1978), pp. 79–81.

7. For a brief study of women's roles in war films see Lawrence H. Suid, GUTS AND GLORY: GREAT AMERICAN WAR FILMS, (Reading, Mass.: Addison-Wesley Publishing Co., 1978), pp. 217-221.

8. The comparison to Hamlet is worthy of further elaboration. Hamlet's "madness" is one of carefully constructed solitude combined with crafty conspiracy with his trusted male friend, Horatio. Only by cutting himself off from the world of sex, love, and social relationships can the Danish prince obtain the false identity necessary for his scheme. And it is precisely his anti-social solitariness that arouses the suspicions of the king—Hamlet's uncle, the murderer of his father, the husband of his mother, and the usurper of the throne—that his nephew is bent on regicide. The male isolate is all too often suspected of harboring anti-social designs; women in general and marriage in particular function to prevent this potential subversion from going too far. For an analysis of Hamlet that concentrates on the strategic interaction of the mysogynist Dane, see Stanford M. Lyman and Marvin B. Scott, THE DRAMA OF SOCIAL REALITY,(New York: Oxford University Press, 1975), pp. 21-42.

9. *Coming Home* (1978) modifies certain aspects of this theme, while lending additional support to others. As an anti-Vietnam War love story, *Coming Home* pits a paraplegic veteran (John Voight) against a thoughtless patriotic marine officer (Bruce Dern) in competition for the love of the latter's wife (Jane Fonda). Although at first this war wife lends modest moral support to her husband's attitudes about the war, she is eventually brought around to an opposed view by her liaison with the wounded marine and her volunteer work in a veteran's hospital. As an Ariadne she provides both sexual and moral support for the adjustment of the paralyzed veteran. When her cuckolded husband commits suicide in despair over his losses—he is painfully stripped of his ideals as well as his wife—she is left free to continue her ministrations to the partially restored cripple to whom she has already committed herself.

10. Deming, *op. cit.,* p. 38.

11. In *Homecoming* (1948), Clark Gable portrays a surgeon who is so ambitious that he neglects his wife (Anne Baxter) and refuses to aid his friend (John Hodiak) in his charitable clinic. Due for a chastisement, Gable goes off to war, distinguishes himself, but falls in love with a nurse (Lana Turner) who dies as a penance for her innocent assault on Gable's marriage and redemption. See Russell Baker, "Golden Oldies," *New York Times Magazine,* May 27, 1979, p. 12.

12. Despite its flaws, anti-climax, and misplaced adaptation of Joseph Conrad's "Heart of Darkness," Francis Ford Coppola's *Apocalypse Now* (1979) captures the fascination with horror that can lead a once ambitious career army officer, Kurtz (Marlon Brando) to desert wife, family, and country.

13. In his otherwise sensitive and insightful study of the films of Alfred Hitchcock, Raymond Durgnat [*THE STRANGE CASE OF ALFRED HITCHCOCK, OR, THE PLAIN MAN'S HITCHCOCK,* (Cambridge: The MIT Press, 1978), pp. 192-195] misses all of these points. By far the best discussion is by Deming, *op. cit.,* pp. 59-64.

14. Haskell, *op. cit.,* p. 223.

15. *Ibid.,* p. 144.

16. Rosen, *op. cit.,* p. 235.

17. Haskell, *op. cit.,* p. 144.

18. *Ibid.,* pp. 180.

19. Rosen, *op. cit.,* p. 307.

20. *Ibid.,* pp. 306-307. See also Carlos Clarens, *AN ILLUSTRATED HISTORY OF THE HORROR FILM,* (New York: G. P. Putnam's Sons, 1967), pp. 102, 144 *et passim.*

21. Deming, *op. cit.,* pp. 39-71

22. Kevin Brownlow, *THE WAR, THE WEST, AND THE WILDERNESS*, (New York: Alfred A. Knopf, 1979).
23. Stanley Cavell, *THE WORLD VIEWED: REFLECTIONS ON THE ONTOLOGY OF FILM*, (New York: The Viking Press, 1971), p. 49.
24. Sigmund Freud, *CIVILIZATION AND ITS DISCONTENTS*, trans. and ed. by James Strachey (New York: W. W. Norton, 1962), p. 24.
25. Cf. John G. Cawelti, *THE SIX-GUN MYSTIQUE*, (Bowling Green: Bowling Green University Popular Press, n.d.), pp. 47–50.
26. Stanley J. Solomon, *BEYOND FORMULA: AMERICAN FILM GENRES*, (New York: Harcourt, Brace, Jovanovich, 1976).
27. Philip French, *WESTERNS: ASPECTS OF A MOVIE GENRE*, rev. edn., (New York: Oxford University Press, 1977), p. 62.
28. George N. Fenin and William K. Everson, *THE WESTERN: FROM SILENTS TO THE SEVENTIES*, (Baltimore: Penguin Books, 1977), pp. 40–41, 209–210, 266–275.
29. Monodrama is that theatrical form in which the psychic components of a single person are decomposed and presented as discrete characters. See the discussion in Lyman and Scott, *op. cit.*, pp. 102–105, 169.
30. Deming, *op. cit.*, p. 152.
31. The Machiavellian themes of *virtu* and *fortuna* and their relation to absurdity are explored in Stanford M. Lyman and Marvin B. Scott, *A SOCIOLOGY OF THE ABSURD*, (New York: Appleton-Century-Crofts; Pacific Palisades: Goodyear Publishers, 1970), pp. 12–27.
32. Jack Shadoian, DREAMS AND DEAD ENDS: THE AMERICAN GANGSTER/CRIME FILM, (Cambridge: MIT Press, 1977).
33. Michael Wood, *AMERICA IN THE MOVIES, OR SANTA MARIA, IT HAD SLIPPED MY MIND*, (New York: Basic Books, 1975), p. 25.
34. *Stagecoach* (1939) is rightly considered a classic of its genre. Beyond formula, however, it symbolically recreates the struggle between civilization and primitivism, but permits an ambiguous ending to that struggle. The Ringo Kid (John Wayne) is an outlaw who in a time of peril to civilization—represented in the film by an Apache assault on the stagecoach that is bringing a thieving banker (Berton Churchill), an effete whiskey salesman (Donald Meek), a Confederate card-shark (John Carradine), an alcoholic physician (Thomas Mitchell), an Army officer's wife (Louise Platt), and a saloon-girl (Claire Trevor) to Lordsburg—rises to heroic proportions and assumes leadership over this motley band of citizens, even though a sheriff (George Bancroft) and the experienced stage driver (Andy Devine) are present. Once in Lordsburg, Ringo kills his enemies, the Plummer Brothers, but having won the love of Dallas, the dance-hall girl ostracized by respectable society, he flees to Mexico with her, to his ranch isolated beyond the reach of American law and society. The sheriff lets Ringo escape. As he and Dallas ride away, the doctor, whose self-respect has been redeemed by his experiences on the journey, exclaims, "Well, they're safe from the blessings of civilization."

* Revised version of a paper presented at the annual meeting of the Modern Language Association, San Francisco, 1979. I am indebted to the helpful comments of Arthur J. Vidich, Charles Simpson, and Cecil Greek.

# Decadence and Modernity in the Unfinished Society: The Latin American Novel

Larry S. Carney

In the early 1970s, Chilean novelist Jose Donoso published his *A Personal History of the "Boom,"* an analysis of the development of the "new" Latin American novel and the extraordinary spread of its reception and influence outside the borders of Latin America itself, especially in the United States and Western Europe. Donoso himself was one of the main contributors to the "boom," most notably through his hallucinogenic confessional, *The Obscene Bird of Night.*

In the 1980s, many Latin American writers speak of the ending of the "boom" and the transition to a new stage of creative experimentation and output by the writers of the region. If the "boom" is indeed over, it reached a culmination in the award of the 1982 Nobel Prize for Literature to Colombian writer, Gabriel Garcia Marquez, author of *One Hundred Years of Solitude* and a number of other novels and short stories, most of them centered on the town of "Macondo," a name Garcia Marquez has chosen to render into fictional narrative and myth his hometown of Aracataca, located in the Caribbean coastal area of Colombia.

The work of Donoso, Garcia Marquez and of other Latin American writers such as the Argentinian Julio Cortázar, the Peruvian Mario Vargas Llosa and the Cubans, Alejo Carpentier and Guillermo Cabrera Infante has been characterized as the expression of "magical realism," an allusion to the 20th century school of painters of the same name. Other writers such as the Mexican Carlos Fuentes, the Argentinian Manuel Puig, and the Cuban Severo Sarduy, whose work may adapt less easily to this label, nevertheless share the imaginative sensibility that Michael Wood has identified as dominant in the contemporary Latin American novel, namely, "a strong sense of reality as fiction."[1]

In Garcia Marquez's novels and stories, for instance, the sense of life, biography, social relations, gossip, tedium and isolation

---

An earlier version of this essay was presented as a paper to the Kyushu American Literature Society meetings, Fukuoka, Japan, June 18, 1983.

The International Journal of Politics, Culture and Society, 1(2), Winter 1987 [291] 101 of the small Colombian town is almost always convincing, vivid, and evocative for any reader acquainted with that reality, either through direct or vicarious experience. The "realism" of his narratives is admirable, both in terms of the skill with which they are crafted and the psychological accessibility of their subjects. Yet time, event, and the boundaries of everyday reality are exploded outward in these narratives, curling back upon themselves to create a dazzling, often terrifying world of myth and miracle. Garcia Marquez's world becomes magical, phantasmagorical, lifted and splayed by the unpredictable powers and forces of the imagination, marvelously and absurdly enlivened by the informing reality and potentialities of language itself. Plants bleed. A priest flies. Human beings live out seemingly endless cycles of being born with lives already completed; sink into decay and dementia without the relief of failed consciousness or death; pursue fantastic dreams that take on the plausibility of the commonplace. The world seems to be controlled by magic; yet at the same time, rendered uncontrollable because it is magical. Characters are indeed the "stuff that dreams are made of," but they are also you and I and, more specifically, the peoples of Garcia Marquez's native land and region, peoples for whom reality itself is often so outsized, so fantastic, so absurd, so menacing, yet prosaic in its very absurdity, that one can comprehend it only by acknowledging its mythical qualities, the dependence of one's very existence on the persistence of physical and human continuities which are, in their essence, folkloric.

*The Autumn of the Patriarch* is Garcia Marquez's narrative of the life of a Latin American dictator, a quintessence of the many and familiar dictators the region has spawned and suffered through the years. The dictator, we are told, dies at an "indefinite age somewhere between 107 and 232 years." During most of this time he shapes and reshapes the world and people around him in the image of his own dementia. He is murderous, cunning, yet disturbingly infantile and innocent in his trickster-like governance of the rotting banana-republic which constitutes his own, but also his people's real yet mythical environment. But does he really die? No one knows, because it seems he has died, yet failed to die, several times before. And if, in fact, he has died, what would be the consequences for the people he has left behind, let alone the generations to follow? To be sure, they have longed for his death and the freedom it would bring. But with his death and the death of the history created by his madness, what is left? Perhaps nothing—or at least nothing those who survive him would recognize or comprehend:

We had even extinguished the last breath of the hopeless hope that someday the repeated and always denied rumor that he had finally succumbed to some one of his many regal illnesses would be true, and yet we didn't believe it now that it was, and not because we really didn't believe it, but because we no longer wanted it to be true, we had ended up not understanding what would become of us without him, what would become of our lives after him.[2]

The "reality as fiction" which is Latin America and from which the new Latin American novel has emerged is the reality of a group of societies which are perpetually unfinished.

They are unfinished, of course, in terms of their rapid transformation and incessant vulnerability to secularization. But all modern societies are unfinished in this sense. Latin American societies are, however, also unfinished at the level of the subjective experience of its peoples, people who see their precarious social environments built and rebuilt, often in whimsical and grotesque fashion, on the rapid decay of previous foundations, on frameworks and supports which bend, stretch, and buckle the new materials attached to them, exposing the sacral order of the past to the devastations of modernity. This twisted and menacingly tottering semblance of order cannot successfully mask the mythic-yet-real dimensions of violence and repression, the vengeance of nature, the terror of the world-out-of-control that are all too often the substance of everyday life in Latin America. Here, the past will not go away, even as it lies dead and decaying across the physical, psychological and social landscape. Here, that which is "modern" and "new" often appears as the obscene and the preposterous, even while it beckons and embraces, entices and envelops, nourishing secular utopian dreams whose terrains and cast of characters become inseparable from those of the other-worldly nightmares the people seek to escape.

Let me illustrate these remarks by a glimpse at the "real" world of Aracataca, the town where Garcia Marquez grew up and the autobiographical staging for what became the mythical structure of the world of "Macondo." Envision the land and the people as they are today: Aracataca is located not far from the shores of the Magdalena River, the muddy current which has been Colombia's historic outlet to the sea. Along this river and along the Caribbean coast toward which it flows, we find much of Colombia's African heritage; the spoilations of slavery, the stubborn resistance and evasion of a proud and inventive black people to the "civilizing" efforts of the colonizer. This is a land of jungle, heat, insects and florid tropical poverty, giving way to dust, solitude and airless winds as it moves inland. To the east, and somewhat to the north of Aracataca, not far from the town and but a few miles inland from the sea, the awesome massif of the Pico Cristobol Colon, the crown of the Sierra Nevada de Santa Marta mountain range rears its snowcovered peak 19,000 feet into the sky. Much of the time the icy crest of this magnificent mountain floats in space, alone and dazzling, its base and shoulders obscured by the haze and mists which hug the seacoast and the tropical lowlands beyond. On the slopes of the mountain and the uplands surrounding it, suspicious Indian cultures harbor their own resentments and socially-hardened resistance to the descendents of the Spanish invader. Catholic churches exist in their towns, but so do the temples and priests of their own religion, a collage of mythic traditions that describes the world and its events as an intricate, precarious balance of forces flowing from the activities of gods and demons who forever overrule the resistance of mere mortals to the fates they impose.

The folklore of outsiders in this region thrives on rumors that these Indians clad in ghostly white costumes hide gold and emeralds in the secret places of their forest homes. But further to the north of the Santa Marta range we find the real Colombian "gold," the delicate green gold of the world's most highly prized marijuana. This along with the "white gold," cocaine, largely grown in the highlands of Bolivia and Peru, but processed in Colombia, has created the "Ricos Nuevos," the new rich, a new class of aggressive, ruthless entrepreneurs, their fortunes built on illicit trade—drugs may now be Colombia's number one export product, outdistancing even its famous coffee—political corruption, and mafia-like gang warfare. Their wealth and power has not only become of immense importance in Colombia, but in the United States as well, especially in Florida, where illegitimate money is turned clean in the buildings and enterprises of legitimate banks, real estate firms, investment companies and factories. In the homeland of Garcia Marquez, the tastes and vices of the American "consumer" create a world where "reality" dangles precariously from a mythical center, a new el Dorado where magical gold is harvested from the earth by peasants or plucked from the coca plants of the Andean plateaus, to be appropriated by the new conquistadores who ride airplanes rather than horses. The archaic reality of deadly pillage and plunder circulates and flowers upon the South American land in modern forms: glistening Lear jets, resort mansions, fabulous hotels, beautiful people of both sexes, banks, computers and the accountant's obeisance to the "bottom line."

But the land is not only used for the cultivation of drugs. Some of the original landholdings of the colonial Spanish exceeded 200,000 acres in size. Still today some family cattle raising enterprises do not fall far short of this figure. Here amidst the proliferation of modern ranching methods and mechanized farming, men still rule other men and women at their whim. Here modern enterprise still views the laborer in ways not too distant from those of the colonial landholder of the distant past: a resource for exploitation whose availability depends on his defenselessness before the law and *de facto* power, and upon his invisibility in the arena of public morality. Vast lands, vast power, and vast poverty; mythical in their proportions and absurdity. Yet you and I could not help but be charmed by the genteel, modern hospitality of any big landowner's home.

Banana plantations, the basis of another of Colombia's export economies, are also found on the Caribbean coast. Today they are in the hands of Colombian businessmen, not those of the United Fruit Company, once the scourge of the region. "Macondo" was a name that Garcia Marquez took from a banana plantation of his youth. Memories of the repression and massacres of banana workers in the late 1920s, the worst of these taking place at about the time of Garcia Marquez's birth, live on in local legend and political consciousness. Today the corporate descendents of United Fruit are not the government-backed *patrons* of the banana country as they once were; but they and other members of the international oligopoly of fruit buyers and distributors still control the organization of the local production of bananas as well as the marketing arrangements which place the fruit on the dinner tables of North America and Europe.

When we think of bananas, sugar, copper, coffee, drugs, or any of the other export commodities which have activated rollercoaster patterns of economic growth and decline in Latin America throughout its history, we realize why the term "boom" to describe the international reception to the Latin American novel in the 1960s and 1970s was chosen advisedly. The booms and busts of the export cycle have fed the Latin American consciousness of "dependency," the acute sense of vulnerability to international economic and political forces over which they have little or no control, but whose consequences for them turn the myth of "modernization" into the theatre of the absurd. The late Alejo Carpentier, the Cuban writer who was the major literary entrepreneur of Latin American "magical realism," captured the dialectic of decadence and modernity, the lived-reality of dependency, in the pages of his novel, *Reasons of State*. He describes a Caribbean nation and its capital city, spirited into the modern consumer economy by the economic blessings (the "boom") of world war, suddenly finding itself suffering economic disaster brought by peace:

> . . . The result of all this was that the new town *decreased*—that is the word: *decreased*—as rapidly as it had increased. What had been large grew smaller, flatter, contracted, as if returning to the clay of its foundations. Suddenly exuding poverty, the city's ambitious skyscrapers—now more like fog-scrapers than skyscrapers—looked smaller as their topmost storeys were deserted, abandoned by companies that had gone bust, and made opaque and gloomy by stains of damp, the sadness of dirty windows, loneliness of statues grown leprous in a few weeks. Unpainted, uncared-for, these buildings combined to make a sort of urban grisaille, which degraded, crippled and decomposed the modern part of the town, swathing it in the decay of what had already been old at the beginning of the century. The porches of the Stock Exchange, half asleep and almost deserted, had been transformed into a market for the sale of singing parrots and turtles, with stalls of salad vegetables and sweet corn, workshops for cobblers and knife-grinders, sellers of prayers and amulets and booths where one could consult healers using mountain herbs . . .

Carpentier contemplates the landscape of dependency; it is phantasmagorical yet very real:

> Abandoned by their contractors, buildings which had not passed the stage of their milk teeth (with incipient walls not yet as high as a man) were to be seen everywhere, ruins of the unborn, presences of what had never existed, permanent beginnings, with roofless drawingrooms, staircases leading nowhere, involuntarily Pompeian columns, while vast urbanization and building-lots in the outskirts had been reconquered by the plants descending from the mountains—plants returning to the capital with their bells and festive plumes; and behind them shrubs, and behind the shrubs trees and tree ferns, all the seedling vegetation of Quick Advance and Quick Growth, shading the small stones among which exiled snakes were beginning to spawn.[4]

And what of the wider political history of Latin America and of Colombia, Garcia Marquez's native land? From 1828 to 1900, 18 civil wars took place in Colombia. The 20th century continued to be marked by continuing violence through the 1930s, 40s, 50s and 60s between the leaders and followers of the traditional political parties. Over 200,000 were killed in the 1950s and 1960s, many macabrely murdered and mutilated in a savage war of peasant against peasant. And still some grew rich as direct result of the slaughter. Lands changed hands and fortunes, some modest, some not, were made through political terror and repression. Today, though governments are elected by vote in Colombia, the army is still a major political force, continuing a brutal decades-old war against guerrillas who live, fight, terrorize and die, committed to the utopian dreams of a better society. For all of this, Colombia is one of the most politically stable countries in Latin America.

All over Latin America, men and women with doctorates from Harvard, Berkeley and Chicago spin econometric models in an effort to manage what has been called "hot house" capitalism. Quite often, their attempts at bringing order are promoted and implemented by the M-16 rifle, napalm and the torture cell. Macondo could not be more fantastic than real life.

Intellectuals and writers in Latin America see all this, experience all this, from a peculiar perspective. Typically they are privileged members of the "exploiter" class, elites trained in an international vernacular. Quite commonly, however, their political sympathies lie with the exploited, whom they sometimes join as political spokesmen and advocates. Yet their access to and ease of movement in the elite circles of their own as well as other countries, is seldom impaired. Their political enemies are often their near and distant relatives, their former and perhaps their present friends. In social class terms, they sit atop a *palacio edificado sobre mierda*—"a palace built upon shit." But their position is not so far up that they cannot see the exposed, distorted superstructure of the palace or smell what its foundations rest upon.

The contemporary Latin American novelist has matured as an artist in a world of literary sensibility shaped by wide acquaintance with the masters of the arts and literature of other tongues—most particularly, the literary and artistic creations of Europe and the United States. In addition to the novels of Dickens, Dos Passos, Joyce, James, Hemingway, and Faulkner, the French, German, but especially the American film have markedly influenced their work. From the writers they have learned technique and the inspiration to discover and release the autonomous power of language. From the film they have also learned technique, but, in addition, a vision as to how the imagination can hold in bold suspension the fragmentary realities of time, experience, and biography. Also from the film—and of immense importance—comes a lively sense of the modern world itself as folklore, a fragile order, woven of fantasies and dreams; fantasies which have dissolved reality into fiction.

The "new" Latin American novel cannot itself be comprehended by or dissolved into sociology. Certainly some of its most characteristic products can plausibly be interpreted as a renewal and extension of the revolution in literature we associate with Joyce, the emergence of the novel-as-language the novel as a self-contained structure or reflexive code of meanings and symbols. Yet, even the most orthodox representatives of this literary line of development among the Latin American vanguard maintain a sense of wonder at the ubiquitous and terrifying combinations of decadence and modernity provided by the history and present predicament of the region. Latin American writers have as a common possession, even as they move onward from the genre of "magical realism," a shared capacity to read and describe their world mythically, and symbolically, one can almost say as literally fictional: to discover in the devices of fiction and the games of language, a way of saying; this is just the way our world is, it is a game of the imagination in which we are the players. But let us never forget the game is real, and the flesh and blood of the players are also real. Macondo is fantastic and deadly. You had better believe it.

Look at the price of real estate on the Florida coast; connect it with the illiterate peasant of the Colombian interior; connect it with the banana on your plate; connect it with the torture cell in the military compound; connect it to the tiny razor hanging from the neck of the partying, fast-track young executive of New York or Los Angeles or Washington; connect it with computer printouts and the towers of international finance; connect it with the banquets of boardrooms and presidential receptions that, viewed from a certain vantage point, appear to be the feasts of assassins; connect it with John Wayne or Rita Hayworth or the attempt to kill Fidel Castro by placing explosives in his cigars. Fantastic?—you had better believe it.

The question remains, then, is it truly the autumn of the patriarch in Latin America: When God distances himself from the world—never did He heal pain, but before He always heard its cry—when He leaves the village, the field and the mountain, abandoning them to the province of more secular faiths and the disillusionments and terrors spawned by the failures of these faiths; when the dictator, the corrupt caudillo, the man who strangely kept hope of redemption alive, as he absorbed the hatred of the people even as he incarnated the myth of patriarchal love; when the leader dies amidst a disintegrating sacral order, what remains and what is to come? Gabriel Garcia Marquez, through one of the narrators of *The Autumn of the Patriarch* gives testimony to the death of the old order, the death of the Leader and the death of the reality and the nightmare he was for the people. But the hope of secular redemption can itself only appear as a myth, the myth of release into a new time, a time when the people will move forward. But to where? Fittingly, here the book ends:

> . . . he had arrived without surprise at the ignominious fiction of commanding without power, of being exalted without glory and of being obeyed without authority when he became convinced in the trail of yellow leaves of his autumn that he had never been master of his power, that he was condemned not to know life except in reverse, condemned to decipher the seams and straighten the threads of the woof and the warp of the tapestry of illusions of reality without suspecting even too late that the only liveable life was one of show, the one we saw from this side which wasn't his general sir, this poor people's side with the trail of yellow leaves of our uncountable years of misfortune and our ungraspable instants of happiness, where love was contaminated by the seeds of death but was all love general sir, where you yourself were only an uncertain vision of pitiful eyes through the dusty peepholes of the window of a train . . . with our never knowing who he was, or what he was like, or even if he was a figment of our imagination, a comic tyrant who never knew where the reverse side was and where the right of this life which we loved with an insatiable passion that you never dared even to imagine out of the fear of knowing what we knew only too well that it was arduous and emphemeral but there wasn't any other, general, because we knew who we were, while he was left never knowing it forever . . . alien to the clamor of the frantic crowds who took to the streets singing hymns of joy at the jubilant news of his death and alien forever more to the music of liberation and the rockets of jubilation and the bells of glory that announced to the world the good news that the uncountable time of eternity had come to an end.[5]

But the time of eternity has not really ended yet in Latin America. It is still there, a firmament, an orb of meaning, penetrated and disrupted by the outward movements of secular time, rendered fragile and moribund by the onslaught of modernity and the terrors and hopes of secular mythologies. But still there.

For the intellectuals of the metropolis, new forms of literary output will flow from Latin America, to be consumed and celebrated as evidence of the cultural "genius" of the region. And this one small victory (or revenge) over the metropolis by the intelligensia of the "dependent" peoples should not be deprecated. But for now, the people of Latin America continue to live, and to suffer, the reality of the fiction.

## Reference Notes

1. Michael Wood. December 9, 1976 "Unhappy Dictators," *New York Review of Books* Vol. xxiii, No. 20: pp. 57-58; 57.
2. Gabriel Garcia Marquez. 1977. *The Autumn of the Patriarch*. New York: Avon Books: 205.
3. Alejo Carpentier. 1976. *Reasons of State*. New York: Alfred A. Knopf: 219.
4. *Ibid.*, 220.
5. Garcia Marquez, 250-251.

# Rebetico: The Music of the Greek Urban Working Class

**Dimitri Monos**

Since its inception in 1821, the Greek nation has looked askance at its own folk tradition because it has been one of material poverty and political subjugation. Greeks generally assumed such a tradition could not contribute to the creation of a robust modern nation, and that it could possibly be an impediment to it. European culture and traditions, on the other hand, represented political power and cultural growth. As a result, political and economic dependence upon the West has been characteristic of all Greek governments since 1832. The need to adjust to this dependence demanded the eclipse of the living traditions of Greek peasants. Toward the end of the 19th century Greeks looked to their European friends and allies for "progress," middle class ideology, technology, educational systems, and fashions.

The emerging Greek middle-classes had concrete economic and other incentives to follow this European orientation. Technology, education and industry constituted the foundation of their class positions, economic opportunities, and middle class way of life. In contrast, the lower social classes, composed of refugees from Asia Minor and peasants who began drifting to the cities, had no direct motive or opportunity to embrace or use Western culture. Out of these social classes emerged a distinctive urban character-type, "the rebetis," who has his own slang, living habits, music and dance. His self-image is that of a man who knows how to live. He enjoys "the beautiful" things—music, dance, good friends, "grass," women—and avoids the demanding constraints of a routine life and a middle class ethos. He bothers no one and he expects no one to interfere with his life (similar in a way to the Nigerian characters known as "guys" and to the "cool cat" of America's black urban ghettos in the late 1950s). Like the socialists, the rebetis condemns as inhuman the living conditions of the working class. But whereas the socialist struggles through union involvement and other activities to fight the capitalist class structure and create a more just social system, the rebetis stoically believes that he cannot effect social change and withdraws into the warm circle of his good friends. His life style, in essence, is the antithesis of and a challenge to middle-class respectability. In this respect, the rebetis life style is a form of heroic personal resistance to the dominant culture and society.[1]

The music of the rebetis—rebetico—assumed an important role in expressing this resistance, and this paper explores the origins, context, and relation of this music to shifting class positions and to international political developments.

Rebetica, the plural of rebetico, made its appearance toward the end of the 19th century in a number of urban centers in Greece and Turkey where Greeks lived. About this time, musical cafes of various levels of sophistication appeared in those centers. The standard type was called *Cafe-Aman*, probably a corruption of the Turkish *Mani Kahvesi*, a cafe where two-to-three singers improvised on verse, often in the form of a dialogue, with free rhythm and melody. To give themselves time to improvise new words, the singers would use the exclamation "Aman, Aman" and, as a result, the songs became known as *amani*. The *amane*, a semi-improvised song in which verses were interspersed with long melismas of the word aman, is recognized as one of the earliest forms of the rebetico.

In the early Greek *cafe-aman*, a table and a few chairs would simply be removed at one end of the cafe when street musicians, some of them gypsies, would wander in, play for a while and then move on. Later, small ensembles call *kumpanias*, made up of musicians playing traditional Greek and Turkish instruments, stayed at the cafe for longer periods of time. At the turn of the century, the instruments of the *kumpanias* included one or more *buzuki*, guitar, *tambour*, the *oud*, and the accordion. Mikis Theodorakis, the internationally known Greek composer, best-known outside of Greece for his score to the film "Zorba the Greek," has tried to analyze the development of the rebetico from Byzantine times. However, we still know very little about the beginnings of this type of music. We are not even sure, as it is generally assumed, that the "rebetico" is of Turkish origin. In fact, it may be derived from the ancient Greek verb, "remvome," which means to be unsteady or to act at random. Gail Holst, who has written a monograph on the topic, remarks that no Turkish scholar has yet come up with a plausible etymology for the word "rebetico" in the Turkish language (Holst, 1982:2). George Giannaris, on the other hand, suggests that it comes from the Moorish name for an early three-gut-string lute, the *rebet* or *rebec*, and, therefore, that it originally referred to things involved with the music and environment of the player of the rebet. Finally, Fevos Anoyiakis satisfies all sides, and is probably most correct, in attributing many elements of the rebetico song to Byzantine and Turkish music, to the music of the Greek countryside, and even to the Italian Candade (Serenade) (Petropoulos, 1968:84).

The Turkish influences on the rebetico, however, are undeniable, as it was developed to a large degree by Greek refugees who left Asia Minor in 1922. These people had lived under Turkish rule for more than 400 years. They spoke Turkish (some did not even speak Greek), had Turkish friends, and lived next door to their Turkish neighbors. Also, they were very musical people, and music is born out of myriad sounds which permeate the air and reach our ears. The wind, the chanting of the Greek vespers, the tones of the Turkish language, the sound of the blacksmith's hammer pounding and shaping a Turkish scimitar, the voice of the Muezin calling the faithful to prayer at sunset—all of these blend to penetrate and shape both our consciousness and the products that sprout from it. After a while, it becomes almost impossible to distinguish which sounds of the song one has just composed are influenced by the Greek chanter or the Turkish Muezin.

Ultimately, of course, it does not really matter, for the music that results is harmonious, soothing, and inspiring. Music, purified of political and religious overtones, is perhaps the only vehicle of communication between politically and religiously antagonistic peoples. Religion or politics raises an angry fist. Music joins and shakes hands and inspires dancing together.

The leading instrument of the rebetico is the *buzuki* and songs and dances associated with it are referred to as rebetic or *buzuki*.[2] The derivation of the word *buzuki* is probably Turkish. In the Turkish language, *bozuk* means broken or small change.

The rebetico song developed in seaports—Piraeus, Constantinople, Smyrna, Thessaloniki—and harbor cities in the Middle East where goods were exchanged and cultural forms confronted one another. The buzuki, therefore, is very similar to the Moorish *rebec* or *rebet*, and the Turkish *saz*.

The *buzuki* is constructed by men of great craftsmanship, using laminated strips of ebony wood in the most expensive models, and with inlays of nacre or ivory. It has three sets of double strings tuned D-A-D, strung from a fretted neck to a bridge on a wooden belly, shaped like a pear-half.

The *buzuki* has traditionally been a solo instrument. When a good musician wants to show his virtuosity, he improvises in the *taximi* (*taqsim* in Arabic), a solo performance or the long solo introduction to a song.

A companion to the *buzuki* is the *baglamas*, a miniature *buzuki* similar to the tiny *tsouras*, played in Turkey. The reason for its size is connected with its function. It was originally designed by inmates of prisons and hideouts during the Ottoman occupation and could be easily hidden and smuggled in. Others carried it in higher places. In his mission to persuade dictator Metaxas to lift the ban he had imposed on the performance of rebetika songs, Yannis Papaioannou, wearing a huge overcoat, smuggled a *baglamas* into Metaxa's office, played for him, and left the presidential office victorious.

The songs of the rebetico music are not based on Western scales. Their foundations are modal types which can be written out in the form of a scale. Their characteristic is that certain relations between notes are emphatically stressed and certain notes are more important than others. Many of these modes are borrowed from Arabic or Turkish music and are called *makams*. In classical Arabic music, there were enough *makams* to express every possible mood, emotion or human yearning. Rebetico musicians changed the name to the Greek word *Thromi*—roads. A few of the refugees from Asia Minor had a rich repertory of these roads (Yovan Tsaus was probably the most knowledgeable), but Holt (1983:66) has concluded that the rebetico repertoire never used more than a dozen of them.

The cultural exchange between Greek and Turkish culture is clearly reflected in the bilingual nature of the rebetico songs, whose lyrics are simple and at times even childish in their lack of sophistication. Turkish words, however, are frequently interspersed in the Greek lyrics. During 400 years of linguistic exchange, Turkish had made inroads into the Greek language. Also, as had been mentioned, since most of the early composers of this type of music were Greek refugees from Asia Minor, it is not surprising that their lyrics contained an abundance of Turkish words. However, even composers who were born in Greece, had never been to Turkey, and did not speak the Turkish language used Turkish words and, more interestingly, images from Turkish life in their lyrics. Thus, even in the songs of the great Vamvakaris, who was born on the Greek island of Syros, and Vassilis Tsitsanis, from the heartland of Greece, we find images and references to Turkish women, belly dancers, and the ease, comfort, and joys of a sultan's harem.[3] This appears to indicate that the common people were nostalgic for that part of their folk culture—the Turkish—from which they had been suddenly and abruptly separated as a result of international political events beyond their control.

The abrupt uprooting and expulsion of the Greeks of Anatolia in 1922 naturally caused a dramatic shift in their social position and status. Many of them had been prosperous merchants and businessmen, or at least were financially comfortable, and now they were faced with abject poverty in the urban slums of Greece. Many found some relief in the *buzuki* music and its milieu, where they were eventually joined by other city dwellers living under similarly wretched conditions.

Since the closing decades of the 19th century, however, rebetico and its social environment had been considered unacceptable and immoral by proper, middle-class people. To those who had turned their cultural compass to the West, rebetico was Turkish and non-Greek, Oriental and non-European and, consequently, useless. Even to conservative people of the lower classes, rebetic music was associated with hashish and other habits thought to be degenerate and immoral.

In his autobiography, one of the great rebetico composers, Yannis Papaioannou, who as a child was expelled with his family from Asia Minor, vividly relates his mother's wrath when he first bought a *buzuki*:

> So I bought my first *buzuki* and took it home. God preserve his servant! My mother's reaction was terrifying. She started yelling and berating me to no end. 'Take it and leave my home you bum, murderer, disgusting creature. You dared bring a *buzuki* into this good house—then, take it and vanish with it from my sight!' Indeed she kicked me out of the house. A mother disowning her child because of a *buzuki*! Can you imagine this? As if it were a killing instrument.

And lovingly he concludes: "My poor, beloved instrument, how much have you also not suffered with the rest of us!" (Papaioannou, 1982:21–22).

Mihalis Yenitsaris encountered a similar reaction when he cut his first record. While there was great jubilation among his friends, his parents felt disgraced. His mother locked herself in her house and would not come out for three days. "You have disgraced us," she kept saying, "we don't dare show our face in the world. Have you no shame, to cut a record—such a shameful thing—and worse, to have the whole world listen to it!" (Hatzidoulis 1976: 136).

Nevertheless, the rebetico became the music of the poorest class of urban workers in Greece, probably because, as Holst (1983) suggests, it was this group of people who were most open to contact with the refugees from Asia Minor and who could freely borrow musical elements from whatever they heard around them. More than this, however, they adopted this music because it related directly to the conditions of their life, as many of these people were similar to the refugees—peasants dispossessed of their lands and forced to eke out a living in the slums of large, alien, urban centers. Their removal from their villages and wretched living conditions were frequently the result of international events—as in the case of the Greeks from Anatolia—or, at times, internal Greek political maneuverings. In any case, the music and songs of the refugees had great appeal to them.

But what is the nature of this type of music?

The rebetico songs are similar, in a way, to the American blues, another musical form that emerged from the depressed, urban lower classes. Their subject matter is "the life surrounding the jilted lover, the outcast, the downtrodden, the wronged, and, of course, the addicts of hashish and other opiates. Their vocabulary and intonation are drawn primarily from the life of the *buzuki*-type man, the anti-hero of sorts, in his poverty, unloved, and going from the life of the fisherman to that of the hashish smoker in life-after-death" (Giannaris, 1972:122).

Three of the basic themes of the rebetis life—the inhumanity of the social system, the undependability of a woman's love, and the comfort of friendship—are reflected in both the lyrics of the rebetico and the expressive forms of its dances.

*Tsifteteli* is a dance for a couple. It was originally a woman's dance, the stepchild of the "belly dance" which originated in the Arab lands and in Turkey and first made its appearance in the harem (Giannaris, 1972:124). The elusive nature of love is suggested strongly in the movements of the dancers. While complete freedom of body movement is allowed, and gyrations strongly suggest sexual desires, the couple never make contact, never touch.

In contrast to the *tsifteteli*, *Hasapikos* (butcher's dance) has specific steps and is danced to a 4/8 (2+2) beat. This dance has its roots at the meat-market in Constantinople (Istanbul) and under Turkish domination it was danced by the Genitzars, an elite Turkish military group frequently recruited from Greek towns. Two or three people hold each other by the shoulders forming a straight line and following a strict set of rules. Due to the strictness of the rules and the intricate step variations, one usually performs this dance with others one knows well. This is a dance of friendship, a homage to the only relationship that a rebetis can trust, then and now. The dancers hold each other with undeniable affection, confidently leaning on and supporting each other with care. (It is the dance performed by Zorba and his intellectual friend at the conclusion of the film *Zorba*.)

Finally, the rebetis's alienation from and contempt for the middle-class ethos is characteristically expressed by the *Zeibekikos*, a dance of strictly solo performance. The Greek-style *Zeibekiko* has its roots in Smyrna, a large seaport of Turkey in the Aegean Sea which was for centuries a center of Greek culture. The dance has no specific steps. It is usually performed by men, and the dancer, always keeping the tempo, creates his own steps based upon his mood and personality. The rhythmic pattern of the dance itself is always the uneven 9/8 (2+2+2+1). A very interesting description of the dance is given by Gail Holst, as she observed it for the first time:

> The solo dance was unlike any dancing I had ever seen—not exuberant, not being done for the joy of movement, not even sensual. It reminded me almost of a Quaker meeting where only if the spirit moves does a man speak. The music would begin, the rhythm insistent, the voice harsh and metallic, and the dancer would rise as if compelled to make a statement. Eyes half-closed, in trance-like absorption, cigarette hanging from his lips, arms outstretched, as if to keep his balance, he would begin to slowly circle. As the dance progressed, the movements would become more complex; there would be sudden feats of agility, swoops to the ground, leaps and twists, but the dancer seemed always to be feeling his way, searching for something, unsteady on his feet. The dance took place in public, people were watching it, and yet it appeared to be a private, introspective experience for the dancer. Sometimes there would be applause for the dance, sometimes not, but the function of the dance was certainly not to entertain the company. It was as if the dance served as a sort of catharsis for the dancer, after which he sat down at his table and continued eating and drinking with renewed appetite (Holst, 1983:11-12).

In developing his distinctive musical style, the rebetis borrowed heavily from two rapidly vanishing musical traditions of the refugee and the Greek peasant. But like all vital cultural forms, rebetico is not simply the new shell of older cultural styles. It is invested with life and vigor by musicians reacting in their own special way to their own experiences and to the specific social and historical context in which they find themselves. Rebetico adapts older musical forms as a cultural response to the anguish, pain and injustice of urban poverty and powerlessness, and as an expression of the needs, interests, and hopes of the urban poor and working classes. Thus, against the political and economic forces which drove them to the cities in the first place and which impose impersonal structures and strictures onto their daily lives, rebetico affirms and celebrates the importance of personal friendship. As an outlet for the frustrations engendered by blocked mobility, thwarted ambition, and economic depression, rebetico exalts the universal soma of love, sex, and, since it is primarily a male musical form, the fickleness of woman. Finally, the *Zeibekiko* enables the dancer to almost ritually purge himself, at least temporarily, of the pent up frustrations created by political and economic as well as personal misfortunes. Functionally, the *Zeibekiko* resembles not so much the Quaker meeting suggested by Holst as it does the old American camp-meeting revivals, in which the availability of salvation provided an opportunity for emotional catharsis. In all these ways, the rebetico and *Zeibekiko* are the cultural responses of a particular group to the changed conditions of their lives. More specifically, they are cultural products of the transformation of the Greek peasantry into an urban working class.

## Notes

1. This statement is based on the theoretical argument presented by Angela Kail in the introduction to the autobiography of the great rebetico composer Markos Vamvakaris. Since I have made a free translation from the Greek text, I have omitted quotation marks, but the idea is Angela Kail's.
2. When, for instance, Greeks say "let's go to the *buzukia*," they mean a place where rebetic music is played.
3. For instance, a song by Tsitanis, titled "Gioul - Bahar" (purely Turkish words), contains the words *havas* and *yavas-yavas* (bit by bit). In another song he uses the Turkish sentence *gioule olsoum*, to become, to happen.

## References

Giannaris, G. (1972). *Mikis Theodorakis: Music and Social Change.* New York: Praeger.
Hatzidoulis, K. (1979). *Rebetiki Istoria.* Athens: Nefeli.

Holst, G. (1983). *Road to Rembetika: Music of a Greek subculture, songs of love, sorrow and hashish.* Athens: Denise Harvey & Co.

Papaioannou, Y. (1982). *Dobra Ke Starata: Aftoviografia.* Athens: Kaktos.

Petropoulos, E. (1968). *Rembetika Tragoudia: Laografiki Erevna.* Athens.

Vellou-Kail, A. (1978). *Markos Vamvakaris: Aftoviografia.* Athens: Papazisis.

# Music and Society in the 20th Century: Georg Lukacs, Ernst Bloch, and Theodor Adorno

**Robert Lilienfeld**

## The New Sociology of Music

The sociology of music, neglected until recently, has begun to attract the labors of many scholars. One chapter in that musical sociology will belong to the writings of Georg Lukacs, Ernst Bloch, and Theodor Adorno. Their writings are interrelated in complex ways; each was influenced by, and opposed to the others. None of them was a musicologist or sociologist in the conventional academic sense; rather, each was an odd mixture of aesthetician, social philosopher, ideologue, and bohemian.[1]

The musical writings of Lukacs, Bloch and Adorno span the period from about 1915 to about 1975; during the period from about 1860 to 1920, western music had undergone revolutionary changes to which these authors responded by developing their own interpretations of the meaning of those changes. Characteristic of their approaches was an attempt to establish relationships between the meaning of music as a cultural form and the social and political structures of Western society. Working from a Marxist point of view, they perceived the major issues affecting the music of their time—the debates over "program music" versus "absolute music," the growing crisis of tonality that overshadowed the second half of the 19th century, and the changing social conditions affecting music and musicians—as less important than certain political and ideological rigidities, these three imposed limits and distortions upon their sociology of music. These usually took the form of broad declarations of the connection between artistic styles and genres, and social changes, which they proclaimed but did not demonstrate, plus frequent lapses into cloudy aesthetic imagery or purely personal polemics. But in addition, they also contributed genuine perceptions and insights.

## The Transition to the 20th Century

Lukacs and Bloch were born in 1885, Adorno in 1903. Thus, each began his studies and life work within the cultural atmosphere of the 19th century, a cultural order that did not end until the war of 1914–1918, and in some areas lingered on well into the 1930s. The 1920s was the decade that witnessed a decisive departure from the culture of the 19th century. The break with the literature and music of the 19th century included such developments as the new forms of poetry in the works of Eliot and Pound, and the formulation, in 1924, of the twelve-tone system of composition by Arnold Schoenberg.

Thus, Lukacs and Bloch came to awareness during a time of transition, but nevertheless a time that remained within the 19th century cultural atmosphere. In retrospect, it might be argued that that period resembles a golden age that reaches its apogee before the descent into cultural emptiness. The plunge into that abyss has been the gift of the 20th century to the world. Adorno's writings, begun somewhat later than those of Lukacs and Bloch, reflect the difference between the two eras. Although brought up in a rich musical heritage, Adorno, even more than Lukacs and Bloch, was willing to do violence to his own experience by a rigid commitment to dialectical fantasies. Nevertheless, in all three there are to be found brilliant observations and theoretical formulations that remain both valid and fruitful.

These men entered a musical world that offered three features which subsequently formed the salient background to their respectively distinctive writings:

1. the struggle between the so-called "absolute music," and "program music."
2. the growing exhaustion of the musical language, known as the crisis of tonality. This crisis began with the chromaticism of Chopin-Liszt-Wagner, continued through the experiments of Debussy-Mahler-Richard Strauss, became much more intense in those of Scriabin, Reger, and Schoenberg, culminating in Stravinsky, Alban Berg, and Anton von Webern. (It should be noted that Adorno studied composition with Alban Berg). What had begun as a common musical language ended in a multiplicity of aesthetic experiments, each introducing a private or cultic vocabulary.

3. changes in the social condition of music and of musicians, and, with these, changes in the character of composing and composers. The rise of avant-garde-ism as an aesthetic attitude influenced not only musical practice, but even more the ways about which these matters were written. Lukacs, Bloch and Adorno were partly influenced by avant-garde-ism, but in part were uncomfortable with the avant-garde. They did not resolve their ambivalence.

## Changing Conceptions of Music in Society

Ancient music had never stood by itself; it was always inseparable from ritual, legend, dance and poetry; its "meaning" was given to it from the outside. But a distinctive feature of western music has been its long struggle to create a music separated from exterior meanings—to develop autonomy. A first step towards this goal was taken with the late medieval development of polyphony and of chordal harmony, and their coordination, the unique features that came to characterize western music. But these developments occurred when Occidental music was still primarily vocal and choral; instrumental music remained rudimentary. A second major step was taken with the emergence of perfected keyboard instruments, systems of tuning, and perfected families of instrumental design, such as the violin family—violin, viola, violoncello and contrabass—and of choirs of wind and brass instruments. These new resources provided the basis on which instrumental music could become autonomous.

Thereafter began the evolution of an abstract art of instrumental music. This long development culminated in the sonata form, brought to early perfection by the "first Vienna school"—Haydn, Mozart and Beethoven. The sonata constituted a *genus* from which sprang the various *species*, including the piano sonata, the string quartet and the other *genres* of chamber music, the concerto, and the symphony, the latter being a sonata for orchestra.

A new language emerged, or rather, music had developed its own language. Musical meanings were now conceived entirely in musical terms; there were forms of musical motion (phrase systems); goals of that motion (various keys); delaying devices (sequences, modulations, variations), and tonal regions within which musical themes and dramas could unfold involving departures, wanderings, and returns.

The instrumental sonata undoubtedly began as a dance suite, that is, as something related to an extra-musical art and social setting; but the dances quickly became more and more abstract and stylized. The minuet survived for a time, but only for a time; it was replaced by the Scherzo, which in turn soon evolved into an abstract instrumental form.

However, while this rich language of absolute or abstract music was being developed, another product of musical thought, program music, was preparing to attack it, and moving to appropriate its language for other purposes.

One trend of musical aesthetics had always claimed that music not only expressed emotions but could evoke them. Fearful soldiers could be made brave by appropriate music, and the same music could strike fear in the hearts of enemy soldiers. The sick could be healed by music, as was King Saul by David's playing of the harp.

Musicians have always imitated natural events in the world: bird songs, storms, animal cries, rain drops. They have composed music for rejoicing and for lamentations. This musical tradition was linked to the musical conceptions of antiquity, equating musical harmonic ratios with the "music of the spheres." Specific musical scales were associated with gods and goddesses, or seasons of the year, or with planets. Ancient literature is full of stories concerning the ability of a great musician to create effects "out of season," by performing music in the scales associated with winter or summer, or to heal the sick, or to make audiences laugh or cry. Music was thought to be a kind of magic. This older conception of music would not surrender easily to absolute music.

The doctrines of the musical Baroque—the *Affektenlehre*—taught that specific musical motives represented specific "affects"—hope, guilt, despair, anger, and the like. It was not clear whether these motives were expressions of these affects, or were symbols of them, or could evoke them, or perhaps all of these. But, by the late 18th century, the *Affektenlehre* had retreated—as had tone-painting in general—in the face of the triumphs of abstract instrumental music. Composers would continue to write program pieces, or, as they were often called, "character pieces," but these were most often regarded as tricks or jokes. Thus, while we listen quite seriously to a Beethoven sonata or symphony, his piece on "Wellington's Victory" (complete with imitations of cannon fire and the like), or on "The Rage Over a Lost Penny" is considered to be a trifle. Increasingly separated from either practicality or the need to justify itself by creating emotional moods, music could claim an intrinsic value in its own right.

The triumph of absolute music can be seen in the contemporary usages of concert life. Today music is performed with a complete disregard for practical occasions. At the same concert one may hear a cantata, a serenade, excerpts from an opera, and dance music. Such mixtures suggest that the intrinsic value of the music transcends its social function, and is best comprehended from a purely musical orientation. A church might advertise that a Bach cantata will be performed at a Sunday service; and one must wonder—as churchmen have worried for generations—whether the church service is being overshadowed by the musical experience.[2]

However, the sovereignty of absolute music was seriously contested. The romantic movement reawakened the older conception of music as an art that was pictorial, evocative and emotive, in all sorts of ways. The early representatives of the new program music included Hector Berlioz, Karl Maria von Weber, and Franz Liszt. Liszt claimed that music could tell a story; moreover, that in telling the story of a hero's life, the composer could depart from formal procedures and create expressive programs more important than symmetry, recapitulation and resolution could provide. The later representatives of this approach, Richard Wagner, Richard Strauss, and Claude Debussy, brought the expressive and programmatic features of music to the forefront. Richard Strauss even boasted that program music had progressed so far that the audience would be able to tell the difference between knife, fork and spoon, in a musical portrayal of a dinner party.

Program music as a movement was attacked in the year 1854, when Eduard Hanslick published his remarkable treatise *On the Beautiful in Music*.[3] Hanslick, the Viennese contemporary of Bruckner, Wagner, Brahms and Mahler, was a formidable figure: the world's first professor of musicology and a powerful critic whose writings are of lasting interest. He was caricatured without mercy by Richard Wagner in his opera, *Die Meistersinger von Nürnberg*, as Beckmesser, a sterile, carping critic. In an early version of the libretto, he had been named "Hans Lich." A critic, Wagner seemed to say, is someone who tells others how their work might be better, but produces no work of his own. Yet Hanslick's essay, though angry and ill-tempered, remains a powerful and brilliant work to this day.

Hanslick pointed out that a piece of music could evoke as many images as there were listeners. Some would "see" in the music a storm at sea; others, a quarrelsome dialogue between lovers; still others might evoke the lamentation of Dido for her lost lover Aeneas, and so on. Hanslick pointed out that many composers— Bach and Handel among them—had used the same music in different operas, or once in an opera and later for a cantata, and he pointed out that the music served equally well for both occasions. He selected a phrase from Gluck's *Orpheus*, set to the words, "I have lost my Eurydice; nothing can equal my grief," and showed that the music could just as easily be sung as, "I have found my Eurydice; nothing can equal my joy." Hanslick's point is powerful, and the example is by no means unique. Josquin des Prez's great composition, set to words from the Gospel in which the angel at the tomb of Jesus announces that "He is risen" (*Tulerunt Dominum meum*), had also been used for the words of King David lamenting the death of his son Absalom (*Lugebat David Absalon*). And, in both settings, the effect was equally powerful. How could the same music serve so well for such different texts? Hanslick, in effect, answered that "program notes" were a kind of libretto without actors that an uneducated audience needed, or expected, in order that it might supply the response desired by the composer. Music by itself could not do this because it was an autonomous language, a self-referring one, one that is separated from specific exterior associations.

The struggle between these opposed points of view was artificially inflated by such musical journalists as Hanslick, Hugo Wolf, and George Bernard Shaw. Wagner was designated as the great representative of "program" music, while Brahms was the leading exemplar of "absolute" music. Although each admired the other's work, their different styles were taken as opposed schools. It was to resolve this kind of debate, at the center of musical aesthetics in the late 19th century (and into the 1920s), that Georg Lukacs dedicated his writings on musical aesthetics.

## Lukacs on Musical Aesthetics

Georg Lukacs often reminded his readers that he was musically untrained, and that he approached musical matters with great caution. His ambitious work on aesthetics, written late in his career, offers only seventy pages on music, while hundreds are devoted to literature and the other arts.⁴ In 1970 he wrote a brief article on Bartok to commemorate the 25th anniversary of Bartok's death. Despite his caution, or perhaps because of it, his few writings on the aesthetics of music show an impressive grasp of philosophical problems, present accurate musical judgments, and provide some genuine innovations.

Lukacs rejected the point of view of the absolutists, the belief that music could generate a world of meanings all its own. That approach could lead to a sterile mathematicization of music. At the same time, he rejected the musical aesthetics of both Wagner and Schopenhauer. Wagner had been inspired by Schopenhauer, the first serious philosopher of music. Schopenhauer regarded music not as the expression of human feelings but of the will to life which permeates all creatures and drives them forward, a blind striving that can be overcome by very few, among them philosophers and great artists. Lukacs argued that music expresses feelings. The composer learns how to mimic feelings and how to evoke them in others. Yet, he need not feel these emotions himself.

> We have seen . . . that music originates from this social and human need, and creates its own unique medium, in order to fulfill this need . . . We see this in the once universal custom of professional mourners (*Klågeweiber*—women hired to weep and wail at funerals) . . . Their mimesis of grief could not only evoke grief in those attending the funeral, but could help them express their grief by breaking through their inhibitions.⁶

Beyond that, the professional mourners stand as an objectification of these feelings, which are experienced in a richer and intensified form. This of course refers not only to grief; the composer learns how to express through mimesis the full range of human emotions. The composer objectifies feelings in all their subjective purity and genuineness. Otherwise they would remain sterile.

Lukacs sought to refute the positions of both Hanslick, on one side, and of Schopenhauer-Wagner on the other, by employing an ingenious argument. Music is a form of knowledge, but not a science; it does not generalize as do the sciences—thus it does not express "universal" or "cosmic" emotions, as Schopenhauer had insisted. Rather, music expresses the logic of the emotions—which do have a logic of their own. That logic can be described independently of either a scientific or a biographical approach.⁷ For Lukacs, music not only expresses the logic of the emotions; it reveals a people's social condition. Unlike Adorno, Lukacs never developed a formal sociology of music, but his sociological perspective appears in his aesthetic writings as a part of his general philosophy.

Lukacs perceived a link between musical expression and the socially conditioned emotions of a people in the debates over the crisis of tonality in western music. We must turn to this briefly.

### The Growing Crisis of Tonality

The harmonic language of classicism had been thoroughly explored by the second half of the 19th century. The harmonic experimentation of the romantic composers led to an increase of expressive, but not of constructive, power. Without the latter, an architecture of large musical structures, which Beethoven had carried to such great heights, began to crumble. A romantic like Chopin or Grieg could produce beautiful miniatures, but not expanded structures. Their very expressiveness not only focused attention on the immediate horizon of the music; it also produced a habituation to the expressive effects themselves. Then a search for newer expressive effects would be undertaken. Eventually, every possibility of consonant and dissonant harmonic combination was explored, with the result that the increase in expressiveness ultimately produced fatigue and indifference. The problem of creating musical motion became ever more salient.

Several generations of composers confronted this problem. First were three born in the 1860s: Gustav Mahler, Claude Debussy, and Richard Strauss. Coming of age in the 1880s and 90s, each responded differently to the exhaustion of the old harmonic language. Mahler made highly original explorations into modal music and melodic development. In his short life he moved music toward a new tonal language, "pantonality." Debussy experimented with the whole-tone scale and with the composition of harmonic textures based on the overtone series. Richard Strauss, trying new and original ways, may have been the first to employ tone-rows—at a time when Arnold Schoenberg was still writing music in imitation of Wagner and Brahms. But Strauss lost his nerve and abandoned his experiments. He did not wish to sacrifice his popularity and so returned to the tonal language of romanticism. The next generation, Alexander Scriabin, Max Reger, and Arnold Schoenberg, all born in the early 1870s, were confronted by the crisis of tonality in a much more intense form. All three were highly gifted and engaged in original experiments. Unfortunately, both Reger and Scriabin died young, in their early forties, and so their work did not crystallize in any usable way. But Arnold Schoenberg (1874-1951) introduced the twelve-tone system, which, however, was slow to be accepted. For the next generation—Bela Bartok, Igor Stravinsky, Alban Berg, and Anton von Webern— the problem of a viable musical idiom was central. The work of each shows a striking series of stylistic inconsistencies and discontinuities. What we witness here is the breakup of the common tonal language into a multiplicity of aesthetic experiments, with each composer trying in a variety of ways to develop a musical idiom. From the beginning of their careers, Berg and Webern associated themselves with Schoenberg's twelve-tone system. Stravinsky, influenced by Rimsky-Korsakov in such early works as the *Firebird*, moved on to an experimental neo-primitivism in the *Sacre du Printemps*; later, he attempted a neo-classical style in such works as *l'Histoire du Soldat*; finally he adopted Schoenberg's twelve-tone style. Only Bela Bartok held aloof from these tendencies. Engaged in stylistic experiments of all kinds, he conducted researches into Hungarian folk music, and followed these with explorations of the folk musics of other peoples. His explorations of the tonal idioms that he found in these folk musics found their way into his own composing with fruitful results. Here, musical and sociological considerations converged.

Lukacs and Adorno did not deal with the crisis of tonality directly; rather, they equated it, rather loosely, with what they believed was the decline of capitalism. For a long time, Adorno dismissed all folkloristic experiments as politically "reactionary" and, therefore, musically worthless; he treated Bartok with a scorn that he was forced to retract later in his career.[8] Lukacs, however, praised Bartok's work with folk idioms, offering some interesting ideas on the relation between folk music and a general tonal language.

## Lukacs on Bartok's Music

Writing in 1970, Lukacs offered a retrospective view of musical and sociological developments.[9] Briefly, his argument runs as follows: the failed revolutions of 1848 left central European nations in a stagnant condition. In Hungary, feudal landowners, in alliance with the newly rising capitalists, jointly exploited both workers and peasants. Artistic and personal development became deformed. Poets and musicians could not openly express themselves. The same was true in Germany. Wagner, who had been a revolutionary in 1848, made his peace with the ruling powers; those who did not gave themselves up either to deep melancholy (Brahms) or to humor and the irony of self-mockery (Fontane). Thomas Mann coined a phrase to describe the prevailing attitude among artists: "'power-protected inwardness" (*Macht-geschützte Innerlichkeit*). Artists were reluctant to grumble or show discontent. In their subject-matter, they emphasized the personal and the intimate as a way to avoid focusing on social, political and economic conditions.

Expressions of discontent did emerge, however, but they took a new form. In Russian literature, Count Tolstoy produced the first portraits of the Russian peasant. In music, it was Bartok who first explored Hungarian folk music, and then went on to explore that of the Czechs, Slovaks, Arabs, Portuguese, and indeed "all folk music." The growing exhaustion of a tonal language based on the triad and the cadential progression led to a search for new resources. Folk music, with its archaic and pre-harmonic traits, suggested itself as having just what was wanted.

Lukacs relates this to social developments: the peasant represented the next turning point in history, just as the bourgeoisie, as portrayed by Rembrandt, had been pictured as an earlier turning point.

"Bartok himself considered the peasants a natural force, and this is why he could ... artistically transcend the artificial alienated human type created by capitalist development."[10] Lukacs related Bartok's later compositions to the same sociological process, and presented a conceptual category for the understanding of this process: *undetermined objectivization*. When social conditions place obstacles in the way of expression, these seemingly insurmountable obstacles actually operate to broaden and deepen the possibilities for artistic expression. What will then emerge Lukacs calls "deep and poignant human emotions through which the beginning of a new era can mean a memorable turning point in the development of the human race. . . ." As examples, Lukacs mentions Tintoretto, Monteverdi, Rembrandt, Goethe, and, finally, Bartok.[11] By undetermined objectivization Lukacs appears to refer to a moment of genuine originality and authentic creation. These critical moments emerge when social conditions weigh upon human emotions sufficiently to evoke new forms of expression.

Lukacs' sociology of music is aesthetic, historical, and philosophic, and, as we can see, not at all empirical or research-oriented. Like Ernst Bloch and Adorno, he often proclaims the social conditioning of music in broad programmatic terms.

### Ernst Bloch on Music and Society

Ernst Bloch carried this sociological perspective even further, asserting that not only musical styles and forms, but even specific composers reflected social conditions:

> The dominance of the melody-carrying upper part and the mobility of the other parts correspond to the rise of the entrepreneur just as the central *cantus firmus* and terraced polyphony corresponded to the hierarchical society. Haydn and Mozart, Handel and Bach, Beethoven and Brahms all had a social mission which was very specific . . . Handel's oratorios reflect, in their proud solemnity, the rise of Imperialist England and her claim to be the chosen people. There would have been no Brahms without the middle class concert society and no musical *neue Sachlichkeit*, no expressionless music, without the enormous increase in alienation, objectification, and reification of late capitalism. It is always the consumer sector and its requirements, the feelings and aims of the ruling class, which are expressed in music. . . .[12]

Bloch draws too facile a parallel between features of society and musical textures. Moreover, Bloch's reduction of such great artists as Handel or Brahms to the status of mouthpieces of a specific social time and place raises obvious objections. If Handel's oratorios reflect only the rise of Imperial England, or Brahms' works only the rise of a German middle class addicted to concert-going, why do their works continue to arouse the admiration and emotions of peoples who are not English, not imperialist, not German, and so on? The experience of these works is not antiquarian, but rather of something living. Clearly there are great artists whose works appeal to distant nations and different cultures. (Why is the Viennese waltz now conquering Japan? Why just at this time?) Furthermore, Lukacs' notion that the artist expresses the emotions of the folk may be out of date. The working classes and peasantries of the world have proven to be more conservative—in a social and artistic sense—than most avant-garde intellectuals ever imagined. Few workers or peasants are to be found at avant-garde music recitals; neither are they listening to nor even pretending to enjoy such works. Nor do they seem to respond to the political dreams of avant-garde intellectuals. In sum, the views put forward by Bloch and Lukacs, that music is both determined by social conditions and at the same time "outstrips" and transcends "a given age and ideology," that it is both captive of the ruling class and yet expressive of the forces that will overthrow the social system, seem based more on their political ideologies and hopes than on any observations of music history.

Bloch has for long been regarded primarily as a controversial Marxist philosopher. Sympathizers regard his work as an original attempt to prevent Marxism from petrifying into an orthodoxy; opponents see it as pseudo-Marxist, romantic and mystic, a symbol of the decomposition of Marxism.[13] His musical writings were completely overlooked until recently. Of the three men under consideration here, his writings are the weightiest and the best, full of brilliant observations on specific composers and on the history and aesthetics of music. His essays on music are not systematic or logical, but poetic and profound, a kind of mood music that cannot be reduced to any logical system of propositions. Scattered among them are observations on the relation of music to society which, while suggesting a close intellectual kinship to both Lukacs and Adorno, add original perspective.

Bloch was a philosopher of utopia and of hope. Utopia was the adumbration of the future that could invade and transform the present despite all resistance. When that happened, there would be a retroactive transformation of many things. A central idea of Bloch was that *what has not yet happened* will reformulate everything once it occurs. Musical expression is a foreshadowing of this, a vicarious emblem of the history that is to be:

> Musical expression . . .is the viceroy for an articulate utterance which goes much further than is currently understood. . .Should visionary hearing of that kind be attained. . .then all music we already know will *later sound and give forth other expressive contents besides those it has had so far*, then the musical expression perceived up to now could seem like a child's stammering toy by comparison. . .*Nobody has yet heard Mozart, Beethoven or Bach as they are really calling*. . .this will only happen much later. . .[14]

For Bloch, music is *the* Utopian art.

I do not know which came first: Bloch's political philosophy or his musical aesthetic. Perhaps they emerged simultaneously and intertwined. But there is no doubt that Bloch saw something in the musical developments of the late 19th century: absolute music was changing from a past- to a future-orientation. Thus, a Bach fugue or a classical sonata showed the unfolding of a theme that had already been stated at its beginning. What came later was the unfolding of potentialities promised in the opening thematic. But slowly this changed, so that what came early had the quality of an anticipation of, a reaching out for, something that was to arrive later. Themes were presented that were fragmentary, nebulous, incomplete, not so much a "being" as a "becoming."

In the early classical symphony or sonata, the first movement had always been deeper, heavier, more profound than the movements that followed. The later movements were lighter, more relaxed, with the finale often being the most light and playful. Mozart and Haydn deepened the second movement—the slow movement (slow as a contrast with the impressive first movement); Beethoven replaced the dance-like minuet (the third movement) with the scherzo, a more ambitious construction. And in his Ninth Symphony he tried but failed to make the finale as profound as what had gone before. Even the finale of his Fifth Symphony, as Berlioz remarked, is a letdown, a disappointment after the thrilling transition from the scherzo.[15]

Schubert, Bruckner, and Mahler struggled to shift the symphony's center of gravity from the first to the last movement. Bruckner never succeeded; the marvelous adagio of his Ninth Symphony exhausted his energies, and he never wrote the finale. Bruckner bequeathed this problem to his disciple, Mahler, who succeeded (as had Brahms in his Fourth Symphony). Thenceforward, the symphonic process was controlled by its future, not its past.

Bloch was among the first theoreticians of this musical change. Like Lukacs, he paints his sociology of music in broad strokes.

Human needs, socially changing tasks, have been behind it ever since the days of the syrinx. It is clear that the means and techniques of so companionable an art are largely determined by the given social conditions, and that society will extend far into the sound-material, which is in no sense self-active or Nature-given. . . . Sonata form. . .presupposes a capitalist dynamics; the multilayered and totally undramatic fugue, a static hierarchical society. So-called atonal music would not have been possible in any other era than that of late bourgeois decline, to which it responded in the form of a bold perplexity. The twelve-note technique. . .would have been inconceivable in the age of free enterprise. . . . Hence each musical form itself and not just its expression depends on the given relationship of men to other men and is a reflex of this.[16]

The difficulty here is the leap from one sphere of meanings to another. Lukacs, Bloch, and Adorno do not see the problem of tonality in its own terms, but only as a symptom of a deeper malaise in the civilization beyond music. They do not grant to composers the authenticity of approaching the musical problem *per se*, an authenticity that might reflect an entirely different kind of experience and attempt at world ordering than that of *litterateurs*. Only Adorno had some sense of the autonomy or authenticity of musical problems, and perceived that their resolution might be expressed and resolved in strictly musical, rather than socio-political, terms. However, in Adorno this sense was more often than not overshadowed by his ideological commitments and philosophical rigidities.

## Adorno: the Musician as Intellectual

Theodor Adorno (1903–1969) studied music, sociology, and philosophy and was active in all three fields. He composed music and performed as a jazz pianist; he served as close musical adviser to Thomas Mann when Mann was writing his novel about a modern composer, *Doctor Faustus*. Of the three, Adorno was the most highly trained musically (Bloch was reportedly a competent pianist and at one time considered musical composition; Lukacs appears to have been musically untrained), and he was the only one to attempt a systematic sociology of music.[17] With Max Horkheimer, Adorno was a principal founder of what is called the Frankfurt School, and, as such, a spiritual father of the contemporary New Left.

### Composer, Performer, Audience

The separation of composer, performer, and audience that we now take for granted would have seemed strange to the ancients. Music was something improvised *by a community*, by embellishing and decorating pre-existent melodies and scales which had no "composers," or only mythical ones like Apollo or Orpheus.

But in medieval Europe, something new emerged: a polyphonic texture of multiple melodies unfolding at once. An entirely new form of musical notation was evolved, one that could capture not only the spatial relations of these melodies, but also the temporal durations of their tones; time was now captured by a new symbolism. Only now could there emerge a new craftsman, the composer, who had not only to master the art of combining these multiple melodies, but even more, that of writing them in the new system of notation. Even then, compositions served as decorations and elaborations of pre-existent materials, the Gregorian chants. Only slowly did the idea of a composition that was original emerge: the *res facta*, a thing that had been made, rather than had been improvised. (The lingering of the ancient practice of improvising around pre-existent melodies known to an entire community can be pointed out in two areas: first, the Lutheran chorale. J. S. Bach's chorale preludes are musical meditations improvised at the organ on the message of the hymn to be sung by the congregation. Second: American jazz, at least in its early phases, was a jaunty improvisation on successful popular tunes known by heart to a wide audience. There was a direct descent from the first to the second of these practices.)

Although the composer emerged as master of this new technique, he was for long seen as a craftsman. Composers were never only composers; they were also—and perhaps primarily—performers, choirmasters, copyists, and instrument makers. Johann Sebastian Bach not only wrote music; he also performed on keyboard instruments, built organs, engraved and printed music, and he showed great interest in new instrumental designs such as the new (and rudimentary) pianoforte, and made suggestions for its improvement to its pioneers. But this older social role of the musician as master craftsman began to be eclipsed, replaced by the composer as intellectual.

In this respect, Beethoven was an unfortunate influence. His deafness forced him to give up piano recitals and conducting, and to live by composing alone. Because of his stature as a creative artist, he succeeded. But, unintentionally he created an unhealthy model: younger men began to think of the composer as a lonely, isolated spiritual giant who did not have to bother with performing before audiences. The romantic movement, which made high claims for art as source and expression of wisdom as profound as that offered by science or philosophy, assisted in this development. New composers emerged who could not perform at all on the professional level; at present, there are even many who depend on others to orchestrate their compositions. Now began also the separation of composer not only from his audience, but also from the performer. In the classical period, it would normally be the composer who first presented his works to the world, as Mozart did with his piano concertos. And in such figures as Mozart and Beethoven, performer and composer were not only one and the same, but were of equal stature (as was true, later, of Chopin and Brahms). But in the romantic period there began to emerge a new type of performer, the sensational virtuoso, in whom the element of composition might still exist (as with Liszt or Paganini), though secondary to the performer's virtuoso fireworks, or in whom the talent for composition is either very weak, or left undeveloped, as in countless performers and conductors in our own time. The alienation of our contemporary composer from the performer (and from the disciplined skills of the performer) is expressed by such figures as Ravel, a rather indifferent performer of his own works, and even more by the vogue today for composition by electronic devices which bypass the performer altogether. Composers today speak of being liberated from musical instruments, "those museum pieces," and from the tyranny of the star performer or conductor, who may or may not bother to even examine, much less perform, new works.

The alienation of composer from audience also began at this time. By the late 19th century, the aristocratic and churchly support of musicians was fading, increasingly supplanted by a new concert industry based upon mass audiences and later on recording companies. The newer composers dismissed these new mass audiences as "philistines"—i.e., those who welcome only what is familiar and poses no problems for the understanding. (It was Robert Schumann, not only a romantic composer but also a gifted musical critic and journalist, who first formulated the opposition between "us"—the brave band of "Davids"—and "them"—the "Philistines" who welcome only the old familiar pieces.) Increasingly, composers began to write not for audiences but for one another. Between composers and audiences a new element emerged: the journalist and critic who acted as mediator between the audience and the creative and performing artist. Deprived of the older forms of sponsorship—courts, churches and municipalities—the composer had to relate himself to the new commercial concert and recording industries, and to ingratiate himself to the new cultural and state bureaucracies that undertook to sponsor—

and control—the arts. More recently, the emergence of bureaucratic colleges and universities as art sponsors has operated to increase the separatist tendencies of composers. A Haydn or a Beethoven were expected by their aristocratic sponsors—often quite perceptive musically—to be both original and intelligible. But a modern composer, isolated from musically educated communities, is tempted either to write music that is superficially striking and pleasing, and so, he hopes, popular, or to demonstrate his originality and skill by compositional displays of erudition for the benefit of his professional colleagues. Often the two impulses are visible in different works of the same composer.

We see the metamorphosis of the composer from a craftsman responsible to a community into an intellectual who adopts the stance of avant-garde-ism, engaging in experiments deliberately intended to be incomprehensible or repellent. The composer can still proclaim his compassion for the oppressed: music must be ugly, he will say; how else express the ugliness of the age? And we see this metamorphosis as the mark of the 20th century.

This is the background against which Adorno developed his sociology and aesthetics of music. Lukacs, Bloch, and Adorno were, in many respects, romantics. As such, they inherited that claim for art as wisdom first put forward by Schelling and Schopenhauer. Their writings assume that the arts, and especially music, are somehow integral to the whole of society. For Adorno, the central fact of his world was the era of the Nazi death camps. From this horror and from his despair over the post-war world, which had failed to deliver the revolution, he developed an aesthetic and a philosophy of supreme pessimism. His total pessimism was intended as a direct challenge to Ernst Bloch and his philosophy of hope,[19] and his glorification of Schoenberg's twelve-tone system was aimed against the folkloristic and populist explorations of Mahler, Janacek and Bartok, who were praised by Lukacs. Thus, he also opposed Lukacs' musical aesthetic. (The personal and intellectual relations between the three are very complicated indeed, and scholars are only now beginning to examine them. Often, it appears, a slighting allusion to a composer may really be aimed by one of this trio towards any other. In addition, Adorno's insistence that only a sociologist who also had a professional musical training could be reliable as a sociologist of music, while probably true, was just as probably aimed at Lukacs.)

Briefly, Adorno's musical sociology shows the following major features:[20]

(1) Adorno opposed the dominance of the culture industry that had transformed music into a commodity. Although anyone walking down the street might be heard whistling a theme of Mozart or Beethoven, his was a completely passive sense of this music. He would make no attempt to understand the formal transitions and relations between the various parts—its architecture—he would only greet the familiar tunes when they returned. Thus, the culture industry had captured the great works of the past and reduced them to commodities, best sellers, admired but not really understood.

(2) Accordingly, he rejected any sociology of music that took the form of market research, making musical interests comparable to the popularity of brands of soap or cigarettes.

(3) To counter the culture industry, Adorno demanded that modern music forcibly reject the masterworks of the past by destroying their musical language. The weapon for this destruction was to be Schoenberg's twelve-tone system, which would obliterate harmonies, scales, keys, cadences, as well as the intelligible presentation of musical themes. Especially to be done away with was the old distinction between consonance and dissonance. To this end, Adorno seemed completely opposed to the composer's use of "identification patterns;" for this same reason, he rejected all forms of popular music. Here, Adorno aligned himself with certain forms of the avant-garde.

(4) Adorno recognized the importance of the critic. A new mass audience, eager for music but uncertain of its tastes or judgment, and wanting authoritative guidance, relied on the critic, who, through his reviews, exercised a power of life or death over composers and performers. The routinization of criticism has produced the contemporary condition, wherein the arts are dominated by a falsifying publicity, the artificial inflation of reputations and the eclipse of genuine artists. (Claude Debussy's musical journalism contributed to this development. His way of writing has been imitated by countless journalists. The tone and language of his writing is that of a languid young *décadent*, bored by everything, but especially by the masterworks. Since Debussy's time criticism has become a pseudo-art, full of pretentious jargon

of all kinds—sociological, aesthetic, psychoanalytic—to which Adorno himself made major contributions.)

(5) The gulf between popular and high art was something which Adorno saw as created and maintained by "the system," and had to be bridged. Composers like Haydn and Mozart had had the popular touch, as did Johann Strauss. But the commodification of popular music had reduced it to a "depraved. . . .mindlessness defending the existing system," whose defining traits were banality and vulgarity. Popular music could actually "maim the consciousness of those exposed to it." Adorno described the composers of operettas as producing a kind of musical "ready-to-wear," and claimed to see a connection between this attitude towards musical substance and such American shows as *Pins and Needles* and *The Pajama Game*.[21] Especially exasperating to Adorno was the condition that popular art relied on standardized patterns of identification (as if the high art of classical music did not do so; what did he consider to be the function of recognizable themes, cadential patterns, modulating chords, and the rest?). Adorno's contempt for popular music and jazz has recently aroused much critical comment, and he has been reproached for his mandarin-like attitude toward popular art, which he dismissed as *kitsch*. Yet he was of two minds about it; he grudgingly conceded that American popular songs often exhibit "beautifully arched melodies" and pregnant turns of phrase and of harmony, and that some popular songs retained their charm for many years. These he called "the evergreens," why they existed was unclear to him, and needed study, But, he hastily added, popular music was "objectively untrue" and therefore harmful.[22]

(6) Adorno's musical aesthetics were governed entirely by his political views. He conceived the latter in simplistic terms: what he chose to call "Fascism" was struggling against what he called "socialism." He never considered that all sorts of other political and social forms and struggles might exist. In accordance with his politicized vision relating music to social conditions, Adorno identified Schoenberg's twelve-tone system with the forces of progress and revolution, and Stravinsky's style of composing with fascism and reaction. Moreover, he misjudged Bartok's efforts to reconcile folklorism to certain features of Stravinsky's style, especially the neo-classic elements. Adorno's simplistic aesthetic of

opposition exposed itself to serious difficulties. First, Stravinsky's adoption of the twelve-tone technique proved a major embarrassment. Second, as the value of Bartok's work became undeniable with the passage of time, Adorno tried to cover his tracks surreptitiously. However, Lukacs launched a scathing attack on Adorno for his earlier misreading:

> It was no accident that Adorno, whose musical theory postulated Schoenberg's standpoint as the only one leading to salvation, saw something suspicious in Bartok's folkloristic approach. Such persons would quite naturally shrink from the truly great innovator whose truly revolutionary attitude blew up the human foundations underlying the merely formal innovations.[23]

Despite the somewhat overblown language (did Bartok, merely by writing music, really "blow up" human foundations? How? Furthermore, it has to be said that Bartok's work was very uneven; in it are to be found many fruitless experiments, along with some masterworks), Lukacs' judgment of Bartok's significance is more accurate than Adorno's contemptuous dismissal—and he was later forced to modify his stance.

Because music was seen almost wholly in political terms, Wagner posed an insoluble difficulty for Adorno. On the one hand, Wagner was perceived as a theorist of racism and antisemitism, a crude and vulgar thinker, a forerunner of Nazism. Yet Wagner was a powerful and original musical personality, and above all, a precursor of Schoenberg: without Wagner, there would have been no Schoenberg.

In his book, *In Search of Wagner*, written in 1937-38,[24] Adorno chose to dissect Wagner using the weapons of both psychoanalysis and Marxism. According to his Marxian sociology, "Wagner was an impressionist *malgré lui*, as is only to be expected in view of the backward state of the technical and human forces of production and hence too of aesthetic doctrine in Germany in the middle of the 19th century. . . ." Wagner, without being aware of it, had expressed "the unity of the productive forces of the age." His treatment of musical themes was analogous to labor on an industrial assembly line.

> Wagner's work comes close to the consumer goods of the 19th century which knew no greater ambition than to conceal any sign of the work that went into them, perhaps because any such traces reminded people too vehemently of the appropriation of the labour of others, of an injustice that could still be felt. . . .[25]

There is not much reasoned argument in this kind of polemical writing; rather, cloudy imagery works to dissolve men and their musical works into the scenery of social forces. Thus the forces of production generate Wagner's musical aesthetic *and* his librettos *and* his music; they even generate those musical innovations which, without Wagner's knowing or intending, would lead to Schoenberg. Wagner, in effect, is banished from his own lifework. Adorno attributes to him all sorts of motives, impulses, and hidden instincts, which are clear to Adorno but would make Wagner unrecognizable to himself.

Adorno's assault on Wagner also appears to have been part of his quarrel with Lukacs and Bloch, and designed to attack Bloch's more favorable and sympathetic writings on Wagner. Where Adorno gave himself over to reductive "explanations" that sought Wagner's destruction, Bloch approached the latter's work by way of poetic descriptions, a much more difficult task.[26] A detailed comparison of the two men's views of Wagner should interest both aestheticians and sociologists of music.

*The Avant-Garde Intellectuals.*   These three gifted men created a sociology of music out of their political and Marxian styles of thought. Their musicological writings offer a series of keen aesthetic judgments on specific artists, as well as accurate perceptions of the relation between music and society, mixed with cloudy declarations of how the relations of production generate musical styles and genres. All three want to have it both ways: music is integral to society, a social product; and yet music is revolutionary, can blow up the foundations of the existing order (Lukacs), is "a kind of analogue . . . to social theory" (Adorno), and is created in advance for another kind of society, thereby helping to bring about that new society (Bloch). All three foreshadowed the cultural politics of the New Left, or perhaps only that which appeared after the collapse of the New Left; the idea of salvation through culture had a brief run during the post-1960s hangover.

In addition, all three exhibited the dialectical hocus-pocus that employs paradox in place of either thought or research. Of the three, Adorno is the most self-indulgent in this respect. His writings are laden with paradoxes. A few examples:

Art aids enlightenment only by opposing obscurity to false clarity; then it shows its own darkness. . . .[27]

The inhumanity of art must triumph over the inhumanity of the world for the sake of the humane. . . .[28]
Music is doomed, but this historical process in turn restores it to a position of justice and paradoxically grants it a chance to continue its existence. The decline of art in a false order is itself false.[29]
Art would perhaps be authentic only when it had totally rid itself of the idea of authenticity.[30]

I have attempted a parody of his idiom:

For Adorno to write doublethink both before and after Orwell invented doublethink—which not Orwell but the paradox of the age created through Orwell—is an achievement which barely manages to hide its own lack of achievement.

*The Theory of the Avant-Garde.* This was the title of a remarkable work by Renato Poggioli.[31] The author traced the changing historical meanings of avant-garde-ism. It began with an "alliance between political and artistic radicalism," but then evolved into a kind of dialectic of opposition to whatever styles happen to prevail at a given time. Poggioli labels this *antagonism*: not only to tradition but also to the public. The artistic sect and movement becomes a caste. Because of this the modern artist becomes free-floating (declassed), and can alternate between two postures, "now plebeian and now aristocratic, now 'dandy' and now 'bohemian' . . . ," each status being "equal and opposite manifestations of an identical state of mind and social situation." It was precisely this bohemian spirit, Poggioli pointed out, that provoked all the external manifestations of avant-garde antagonism toward the public.

From this, avant-garde art moved to other views: *"down-with-the past"* (in Italian, *antipassatismo*), which quickly became futurism and the glorification of the machine; *nihilism*, which took many forms, *dadaism* and other forms of obscurantism foremost; *agonism*, a kind of hoping and striving for catastrophe; *experimentalism* and, of course, *alienation*.

It seems clear that Lukacs, Bloch, and Adorno were each, in one way or another, influenced by avant-garde-ism, and hoped to enlist it for their political purposes. But although they trained the powerful weapons of sociological and cultural criticism against others, they did not sufficiently examine their own roots in the avant-garde movement. Adorno especially appears to have tried to make these avant-garde traits into a permanent, frozen, even timeless, feature of his aesthetic. Poggioli remarks that Georg Lukacs "never directly faced the particular problem of the avant-garde." He treated it only in passing:

> He is inclined in fact to attribute an exclusively negative value to the concept of the avant-garde. The only form of modern art which seems to him to anticipate the future, or to be, as he himself would put it, progressive, remains the surviving—and sometimes the outlived—realistic tradition, always the primary object of his inquiries. Lukacs himself assigns the task of judging the seeds of the future in today's art not to contemporary criticism but to future history. . . .
> Surely there is an element of truth in the claim that the avant-gardistic quality of a given work of art . . . can only be perceived by some future consciousness. We might say that no ambitious critic can make do without yielding to the appeal of a futuristic utopia. But it is neither fair nor precise to limit the progressiveness of art to a single type of content (Marxist sociology) and to a single style (realistic narrative).[32]

Thus we see that Georg Lukacs stands in a peculiar half-relationship to avant-garde-ism, being in one sense future-oriented but also closely tied to the tradition of realistic narrative. Perhaps it is this dual, Janus-like stance that made him so cautious in his approach to the least realistic of the arts, music.

Adorno stands much closer to the avant-garde. There is a sentence in his *Philosophy of Modern Music* that suggests a possible clarification:

> Music is inextricably bound up with what Clement Greenberg called the division of all art into kitsch and the avant-garde, which is cut off from official culture. The philosophy of music is today possible only as the philosophy of modern music. The only hope is that this culture will herald its own demise: it only contributes to the advancement of barbarism. . . .[33]

There are certain elements of truth in Adorno's words. Art has indeed been divided into "kitsch"—manufactured culture treated like plastic souvenirs (such as melodies from Chopin and Tschaikovsky made into popular love-songs)—and into the avant-garde. But despite this Adorno has here missed some important things:

(1) The two attitudes—the production of kitsch and the production of avant-garde complexities—can co-exist in the

same artist's mind (Consider Schoenberg's *Verklärte Nacht*: a monument of kitsch drenched in syrup! And much the same can be said of Prokofieff's *Peter and the Wolf* or his *Classical Symphony*, alongside the dissonant complexities of works like his *Third Piano Concerto*.)

(2) Adorno disregards the genuine elements in popular music. American popular song from about 1900 to 1950 was unique, the only music to have had a worldwide response.

(3) If we drop the unpleasant word *kitsch*, and refer instead to popular or populist or folkish elements in art, we can see that many artists show, in their work, an uncomfortable mixture of two disparate elements: the folks elements on one side, and avant-garde experimentation on the other. We find this in Mahler, in Bartok, in Chagall, and countless others. The struggle to reconcile these elements, not always successful, appears to be an important element in the arts of at least the last hundred years. Artists resorted to these two very different resources in their struggle to escape from the styles and themes of "mainstream," "bourgeois," or "academic" art (these are admittedly not satisfactory terms). Perhaps the best way of describing what these artists have opposed is to say that works of art that have proved of enduring merit have come to be regarded as forming a tradition, and it is to this that the avant-garde has been opposed, rather than to any specific artistic school or style. More than this, they have seen a body of critics and academics emerge who have become the self-appointed guardians of "tradition," as though they were the guardians of a great but invisible museum of culture.

### Conclusion

The avant-garde has defined itself not only by what it has opposed; it has come to show a specific content and character best shown in Poggioli's masterful portrait. Lukacs-Bloch-Adorno stood in a complex but unclarified relation to the avant-garde; their failure to clarify this relation constitutes a limitation on their sociology of music. One wishes for a new Max Weber to put their broad statements to some kind of historical test. However, the condition of music today calls for a different kind of sociology than they produced; the fragmentation of music into a multiplicity of styles and audiences, the cornucopia of choices that make available almost all musics from all eras throughout the world, the specialization and fragmentation of audiences for the classics, for avant-garde experiments, for folk music, ethnic musics, for rock, punk, and whatever else, the co-existence of more than one style of composition, all require a sociology of music that is not encompassed by a single philosophical approach.

## Reference Notes

1. This is a revised version of a paper read at the conference on *Georg Lukacs and His World*, held at the Universidad Autonoma Metropolitana, Xochimilco, Mexico, on 19 November 1985. I wish to thank Zoltan Tar for many valuable suggestions during the development of this paper.
2. A few examples of the chronic concern of churchmen over music and its place in the liturgy: Gustave Reese quotes Erasmus, who had voiced "a feeling that was growing ever more widespread": *We have introduced an artificial and theatrical music into the church, a bawling and agitation of various voices, such as I believe had never been heard in the theatres of the Greeks and Romans. . . .The people run into the churches as if they were theatres, for the sake of the sensuous charm of the ear.*
   A generation later, the Council of Trent (1545-1565), convened to deal with the problems raised by the new Protestantism, also had to consider the use of music in the church. Their document of 1562 set limits to the elaborateness of musical settings of the liturgy. The movement towards musical austerity almost led to the abolition of polyphony in sacred music.
   This episode was given fictional treatment in Hans Pfitzner's opera, *Palestrina* (1917). According to the legend, the beauty and simplicity of his setting of the Mass saved the day for polyphonic composition. Actually, it appears that Palestrina's role in the deliberations was relatively modest. Reese recounts: "Duke Albert V of Bavaria, who had just recently acquired Lassus as his *Kapellmeister* and who maintained the most brilliant musical establishment in Europe, exercised considerable influence, as shown by extensive correspondence between him and Cardinal Vitelozzo, in bringing about the ultimate triumph of polyphonic music, pruned to accord with ecclesiastical and humanistic ideals." That the problem continued in one form or another is suggested by later documents on music in the liturgy: the Papal Encyclical of 1749 and the Motu Proprio of 1903. Gustave Reese: *Music in the Renaissance*, Revised Edition (New York, Norton, 1959), pp. 448-450.
   The problem was also found in the Protestant churches. J. S. Bach's troubled relations with his employers at the Thomaskirche in Leipzig, who considered his music much too elaborate, too long, and too difficult for the available choirsingers, are well known. Manfred Bukofzer, *Music in the Baroque Era* (New York, Norton, 1947), pp. 291-2. *The Bach Reader*, edited by Hans T. David and Arthur Mendel (New York, Norton, 1945) pp. 119-125, documents the quarrel.
3. Eduard Hanslick, *On the Beautiful in Music*, translated by Gustav Cohen, edited with an introduction by Morris Weitz (New York, Liberal Arts Press, 1957).
4. Georg Lukacs, *Die Eigenart des Aesthetischen*, 2. Halbband (Darmstadt, Luchterhand, 1963), pp. 330-401.
5. Georg Lukacs, "Bela Bartok—On the 25th Anniversary of his Death," *The New Hungarian Quarterly*, Vol. 41, pp. 42-55.

6. Lukacs, *Die Eigenart des Aesthetischen*, pp. 363–4.
7. A recent article by Jacques Barzun offers support for Lukacs' position (it does not appear that Barzun has read Lukacs). Barzun argues that the formal order of music and its expressive order need not be artificially separated, as they are in the quarrel between the advocates of "absolute" versus "program" music. The musician actually follows "a double program, constrained and also helped to create order by two pre-existing patterns that intersect only at certain points. Part of his merit consists in the deftness with which he reconciles the independent demands of the two schemes. The tension between them is a spur to his artistry and technical skill, just as it is a source of the listener's admiration and pleasure."
   Barzun in effect elucidates the logic of the emotions mentioned by Lukacs: "Haydn's 'C major brilliance' would go as well with 'relief after anxiety' or 'indications of innocence after being under a cloud.' This last phrase is chosen on purpose to show how words themselves play upon likenesses that defy analysis. . . .The proof of this is the practice of self-borrowing among the great composers. . . .just in the proportion that music is not literal, denotative, it can connote the essence of diverse experiences." Jacques Barzun, "The Meaning of Meaning in Music: Berlioz Once More," *The Musical Quarterly*, Vol. LXVI, No. 1, January 1980, pp. 1–20. See pp. 5–6 and 16–17, respectively, for the quoted passages.
8. G. Lukacs, *Die Eigenart des Aesthetischen*, p. 393. See also the interesting essay by Ferenc Feher, "Negative Philosophy of Music: Positive Results," in *Foundations of the Frankfurt School of Social Research*, edited by Judith Marcus and Zoltan Tar (New Brunswick, New Jersey, Transaction Books, 1984), pp. 193–205; specifically, pp. 204–5. ". . . .we can understand Adorno's great blunder in the Bartok question. His identification of all forms of the popular with *völkisch* and his unappeasable suspicion of pseudocollectivity behind every collective solution biased his view of Bartok's genius. He simply did not comprehend that it is possible to have a single synthesis of musical material and conception that is both provincially exotic and at the same time guided by world-historical considerations. . . .Nevertheless this author shares the growing opinion that Bartok created a complete and *aere perennius* work, but that he did not open up a new path for musical development in general. . . .Guided by a profound skepticism toward all collective action, Adorno could not understand Bartok's singular accomplishment. Similarly, as a result of his aversion to the miseries of torn and degraded individuality, Lukacs remained unappreciative of Kafka's singular accomplishment."
9. G. Lukacs, "Bela Bartok. . . ." pp. 51, 55.
10. *Ibid.* p. 51.
11. *Ibid.*
12. Ernst Bloch, *Essays on the Philosophy of Music*, tran. Peter Palmer (Cambridge & New York, Cambridge University Press, 1984), pp. 200–201. The reader who is not musically trained might find Bloch's first sentence, and the allusion to *neue Sachlichkeit*, a bit obscure. When instrumental music and chordal harmony came to the fore in the 17th and 18th centuries, much of the musical texture came to be a two-part polarity between melody and supporting bass, with subordinate inner parts to fill in the harmony. This texture was more or less dominant from the late Baroque era onward (Bach's polyphonic music, which his contemporaries regarded as archaic, was an exception). This texture had been preceded by a medieval-renaissance polyphonic texture in which melodic action was dispersed among all the voices, and in which a single voice carried a pre-existent melody, the cantus firmus (or "given melody"). The cantus firmus was originally based on plain-chant, but later secular melodies were also utilized.

The phrase *Neue Sachlichkeit* ("new objectivity") refers to the deliberately cold, affectless music of the 1920s, created as a reaction against the overheated lush romanticism of the late 19th century.

Publication of this work in a generally excellent translation and with a valuable introduction by David Drew is an important event. But I must report an error of translation on page 106: there are no such things as "major" fifths or "minor" fourths; the correct translation would be "upper fifth" or "lower fourth." See p. 127 of the German edition (Ernst Bloch, *Zur Philosophie der Musik*, Frankfurt, Suhrkamp, 1974).

13. *Ibid.*, pp. xvi ff., offers a helpful discussion by David Drew of some of the principal opponents (L. Kolakowski especially) and defenders of Bloch.
14. *Ibid.*, p. 207.
15. *Ibid.*, pp. 40–41, offers a partial discussion of this issue.
16. *Ibid.*, p. 209.
17. See Adorno's *Introduction to the Sociology of Music*, trans. E. B. Ashton (New York, Seabury Press-Continuum Books, 1976). His *Philosophy of Modern Music*, trans. Anne G. Mitchell and Wesley V. Blomster, (New York, Seabury-Continuum, 1973), though more aesthetics than anything else, offers sociological observations throughout. Other writings such as his *Dissonanzen* (Göttingen, 1972), and various scattered essays, are at present untranslated.
18. Adorno, in his *Introduction to the Sociology of Music*, p. 146:
". . . .there really are no more musical partisans in public opinion, like the ones of Gluck and Piccini or of Wagner and Brahms. They have been succeeded by schools squabbling in the cenacle. . . ."
19. David Drew's introduction to Bloch's *Essays*, pp. xxx and xxxiv-xxxv, and xxxviii ff. offers illustrative material.
20. Adorno: *Introduction to the Sociology of Music* is the primary source for these observations. The fact that this book was an outgrowth of a lecture series broadcasted in Germany may account for its unusual clarity. This book offers many excellent observations that lie beyond the scope of this paper; his typology of music listeners is stimulating; his chapter on the relation of conductor to orchestra, which he calls a "phenomenology of recalcitrance," is excellent, as are his observations on concert life. But when he struggles to enforce his political "system," the results are bizarre or disappointing. Thus, the chapter on the avant-garde misses everything. See note 31, below.
21. Ibid., pp. 21ff. This parallel is an instance of Adorno's argument by analogy; there are countless operettas and Broadway musicals *not* set in the garment industry.
22. Ibid., pp. 37–38.
23. Lukacs, "Bela Bartok," p. 54. This may reflect the generational difference between the two men. Ferenc Feher's discussion of this issue is excellent (see n. 8 above). See also: Janos Breuer, "Adorno's Image of Bartok" *The New Hungarian Quarterly* (Spring 1981), pp. 29-35.
24. Theodor Adorno, *In Search of Wagner*, trans. Rodney Livingstone (Thetford, England, NLB, 1981) Verso reprint, 1984). First published as *Versuch Über Wagner*, 1952.
25. *Ibid.*, p. 83. And were there industrial assembly lines in Wagner's Germany?
26. Bloch, *Essays*, III: "Paradoxes and the Pastorale in Wagner's Music."
27. Adorno, *Philosophy of Modern Music*, p. 15.
28. *Ibid.*, p. 132.
29. *Ibid.*, p. 113.
30. *Ibid.*, p. 217.
31. Renato Poggioli, *The Theory of the Avant-Garde*, trans Gerald Fitzgerald (Cambridge, Mass., 1968, Harvard); Harper & Row Reprint, 1971.
32. *Ibid.*, pp. 170-171.
33. Adorno, p. 10.

# Weber and the Rationalization of Music

Ferenc Feher

## Weber's Theory

In analyzing modernity all roads start from and lead to Max Weber. What follows here intends to show that the sociology and philosophy of culture are no exception.

Weber wrote his seminal essay, *The Rational and Social Foundations of Music*, in 1911. It was published a decade later.[1] Although it is a relatively unknown contribution to Weber's epoch-making theoretical edifice, I will seek to show that it exerted a strong 'underground' influence and that it has served as a catalyst for the formulation of both Adorno's and Ernst Bloch's philosophies of music. Weber's dry essay, in which his encyclopaedic knowledge seems to overwhelm the bold theorist in him, can only be properly understood if we place it in its appropriate philosophical context, which is somewhere between Nietzsche and the left-radical cultural criticism of the first half of the twentieth century.

A formal reading might easily give one the misleading impression that in *The Rational and Social Foundations of Music*, Weber reached the zenith of his action theory. Occidental music emerged from an historical battleground on which 'purposively rational' and 'traditionally rational' actions had been contending for centuries. In terms of pure action theory, the ascendancy of Occidental music refers to nothing more than the progressive domination of the field by "purposively rational musical actions" over musical actions of a kind which have only traditional legitimation and which gradually lose out in the conflict. Purposively rational musical actions are offspring of " mathematical reason." Their legitimation derives from the circumstance that the new mathematics, as well as the new physics, could complete the task of reducing the confused kaleidoscope of sounds to mathematically manipulable formulae. Neither Pythagorean nor Christian efforts to mathematize music had been successful due to the overwhelming influence in the Greek and Christian worlds of *ethos* which protected the affective character and blocked the rising hegemony of the consistently quantifiable aspect of music.

The International Journal of Politics, Culture and Society, 1(2), Winter 1987     147 [337]

The philosophical implications of a "strictly sociological" theory are already apparent. Indeed, it is almost impossible to miss Weber's unstated polemic against *The Birth of Tragedy*. For Nietzsche, it was precisely Socratic rationality, the spirit, and the gaze of the antimusical observer of tragedy, that had undermined and ultimately destroyed the Dionysian *qua* the musical and had doomed to failure tragedy as a genre. In turn, both music and tragedy would resurrect, through the anti-Socratic, Aryan, and thoroughly anti-rationalist spirit of German music, the music of Richard Wagner. Weber issued a culturally deep, conservative warning (quoted later) against the Nietzsche-inspired subversive romanticism that threatened his cherished rationalized tonality. The stricture clearly shows that for Weber (mathematical) rationalization was the guardian spirit of Occidental music and that, further, Nietzsche presented for him, at least in this respect, a potential danger.

There is yet another and even broader philosophical implication of Weber's theory of rationalized music. Throughout his life, Weber consistently denied that he had a philosophy of history of his own. However, as many analysts of his work have stated, his sociological action theory was intermittently transformed, in steps imperceptible to the author himself, into a historico-philosophical grounding for and justification of Western modernity with its penchant for separate but equally rationalized spheres, with its battling deities, with its internal tragic dialectic whose poles are the triumphal march of separate spheres of rationalizations, on the one hand, and the disenchantment of the whole rationalized universe on the other. The story of rationalized music is one of the most philosophical chapters in this sociological action theory, which is at the same time a philosophical *plaidoyer* for the Occident as the homeland of rationalization *sui generis*.

What are the terms and the key concepts of the rationalization of music?

The drive toward rationality, that is, the submission of an area of experience to calculable rules, is present here (in Western culture) . . .This drive to reduce artistic creativity to the form of a calculable procedure based on comprehensible principles appears above all in music. Western tone intervals were known and calculated elsewhere. However, rational harmonic music, both counterpoint and harmony and the formation of tone materials on the basis of three triads with the harmonic third, are peculiar to the West. So too is a chromatics and enharmonics interpreted in terms of harmony.

Particular also to the West is the orchestra with its nucleus in the string quartet and organization of ensembles of wind instruments. In the West there appeared a system of notation making possible the composition of modern musical works in a manner impossible otherwise.[2]

Here the basics of the harmonic chord system are described in Weber's own words:

All rationalized music rests upon the octave (vibration ratio of 1:2) and its division into the fifth (2:3) and fourth (3:4) and the successive subdivisions in terms of the formula $\frac{n}{(n+1)}$ for all intervals smaller than the fifth. If one ascends or descends from a tonic in circles first in the octave followed by fifths, fourths, or other successively determined relations, the powers of these divisions can never meet on one and the same tone no matter how long the procedure be continued. . . . .This unalterable state of affairs together with the further fact that the octave is successively divisible only into two unequal intervals, forms the fundamental core of facts for all musical rationalizations. . . . . Fully rationalized harmonic chord music based on this tone material maintains the unity of the scalable tone sequence in terms of the principle of tonality. The unity of the scalable tone sequence is achieved through the tonic and the three primary normal triads any major scale has together with a parallel minor scale, the tonic of which is a minor third lower of the same scalable tone material. . . . . By adding another third to the triad, dissonant seventh chords are formed. . . . . The intervals contained in harmonic triads or their inversions are (either perfect or imperfect) consonances. All other intervals are dissonances. Dissonance is the basic dynamic element of chordal music, motivating the progression from chord to chord. Seventh chords are the typical and simplest dissonances of pure chord music, demanding resolution into triads. In order to relax its inherent tension, the dissonant chord demands resolution into a new chord representing the harmonic base in consonant form.[3]

The focal point and main message of Weber's analysis is to call attention to the sharp contrast between modern (Western) and pre-modern music, that is, between rationalized and far-less-rationalized types of composing music. The latter term, Weber emphasizes, is not totally arbitrary. Several factors, such as the regulative influence of the peculiarities of spoken language, the technical requirements of instruments used for accompaniment and the like, bring recurring but mathematically nonsystematized regularities into pre-modern music. Nonaesthetic (pragmatic and partial) rationalization via *ethos* is exemplified by the 'magical' and 'medicinal' use of music. Weber maintains that, whenever music is used in the service of . . . magical practices it tends to assume the form of rigidly stereotyped magical formulae. The intervals of such magically effective musical formulae are canonized: classified rigidly into right and wrong, perfect and imperfect. . . . . A magical fixing of forms serves rationalization indirectly. For in music as in other areas of life magic may be a powerfully antirational force. But the fixing of intervals serves the purpose of establishing a set of forms against which others are to be tested. In this it may serve as the basis for a uniform musical culture.[4]

Weber never makes mention of this, but it becomes perfectly clear that, although the historical process of rationalizing music has yielded a very peculiar aggregation of purposive rational actions, the net effect of rationalization is something eminently *antipragmatic*. It is music as an *aesthetic* phenomenon, which, having shed all traces of its magical-communal-pragmatic use, arises at the end of the rationalizing process. The Kantian "purposiveness without purpose" has been powerfully vindicated by Weber's philosophically based sociology of music.

"Fully rationalized harmonic chord music" is, however, a dialectical formation *par excellence*. There are several dialectical features of this edifice that have been created by "mathematical" reason, even though the latter seems to be radically antithetical to dialectics of any kind. The first dialectical feature is that systematic rationalization brings us to the limit, the *nec plus ultra* of musical rationality.

The harmonic chord system appears to be a rationally closed unit. However, this is only apparently true. To be representative of its key, the dominant seventh chord should, through its third and seventh of the key, form a major seventh. However, in the minor scale the minor seventh must be chromatically raised in contradiction to what is required by the triad. . . . .This contradiction is not simply melodically produced. . . . .The contradiction is already contained in the harmonic function of the dominant seventh chord itself when applied to the minor scales. . . . .Any dominant seventh chord contains the dissonant diminished triad, starting from the third and forming the major seventh. Both of these kinds of triads are *real revolutionaries* when compared with the harmonically divided fifths. Not since J. S. Bach *could chordal harmony legitimate them* with respect to the facts of music.[5]

A second dialectical feature of fully rationalized music is that, contrary to expectations, it behaves not like a rule-governed artefact but as an organic body which needs the tension caused by an inherently irrational element.

The continuity of progression in the relation of chords to each other cannot be established on purely harmonic grounds. It is melodic in character. Although harmonically conditioned and bound, melody ... is not reducible to harmonic terms ... music could never have consisted entirely or alone of mere columns of thirds, harmonic dissonances, and their resolution. The numerous chords do not grow out of the complications of chainlike progressions alone. They also, and preferably, grow out of melodic needs. Melody can be understood only in terms of intervallic distance and tone proximity. Chord progressions do not rest upon an architecture of thirds. They are not harmonic representatives of a key and not consequently or synonymously reversible. Nor do they find fulfillment through resolution into an entirely new chord but in a chord which characterizes and supplements the key. They are melodic or, seen from the standpoint of chordal harmony, accidental dissonances. . . . .*Without the tensions motivated by the irrationality of melody, no modern music could exist . . . chordal rationalization lives only in continuous tension with melodicism which it can never completely devour.*[6]

A third dialectical feature of fully rationalized music can be summarized as follows: While the music of Western modernity builds on the traditionalist, ethos-based loose regularities of pre-rational music (and, in *uno actu*, it sweeps away the whole antiquated edifice), the inherited traditional rules and their systematic-mathematical rationalization never would have sufficed for the completion of the project. In order to reach its target the system of strict mathematic formulae needed for its counterpart its exact opposite: the eccentric individual, the virtuoso. The writers of the laconic and rich Introduction, who are normally very accurate interpreters of Weber's theory, misinterpret or one-sidedly present Weber's intention at this point. It is undeniably true that experimentation, rather than stereotyping, is the rule with the virtuoso. It is equally true that music addressed to aesthetic and expressive needs (i.e., the music of the virtuoso) may deliberately "savor the bizarre." It is also true that "progressive alterations of intervals in the interest of greater expressiveness," which is the feat of the virtuoso, lead at times "to experimentation with the most irrational microtones."

But it is decidedly a one-sided presentation of Weber's views, as if musical virtuosi, according to him, only constituted "one of the forces eating away the structure of tonality itself."[7] Virtuosi indeed act "irrationally" and subversively but they also have an eminently rationalizing function. In his brief analysis of modern, mathematically-and-fully rationalized instruments, Weber emphasizes that some of the best of these e.g., the Amati violins, could not have been used to full capacity without having been played by the eccentric individual, the virtuoso. This observation can be extended to the works of art themselves. According to the well-known historical anecdote, Beethoven is said to have wept profuse tears of relief, despite his general hostility to the cheap mixing of tears with music, when he heard the young Franz Liszt perform the *Hammerklavier* sonata, a work generally deemed to be unperformable. This illustrates that the virtuoso, a deviation from the rule, was necessary simply for the rationalized work of art to exist.

The theory of rationalized music ends on a decidedly conservative note. The mastery by Occidental music of 'polyvocality' with its three forms—"polysonority" or modern chordal harmony, contrapuntal polyphony, and harmonic homophonic music—has completed the whole edifice of rationalized harmonic chord music. The unsurpassable and canonic period of Western music is seen in J. S. Bach and his age, in which the mastery of "polyvocality" was achieved. Weber warns the musical rebels about the futility of their bold but unconsidered attempts to transcend the limits of tonality and its inherent rationality. A music which is not harmonically rationalized is much more free-moving, Weber admits. It is his firm conviction, however, that the would-be transgressors chase phantoms.

> Our musical sensitivity also is dominated by the interpretation of the tones according to their harmonic provenience. We feel, even 'hear,' in a different fashion the tones which can be identified enharmonically on the instruments according to their chordal significance. Even the most modern developments of music, *which are practically moving toward a destruction of tonality*, show this influence. These modern movements which are at least in part the products of the characteristic, intellectualized romantic turn of our search for the effects of the "interesting," cannot get rid of some residual relations to these fundaments, even if in the form of developing contrasts to them.[8]

Modern music, as it is portrayed in Weber's analysis, bears an acute resemblance to all the dominant features that otherwise characterize Western modernity in his larger narrative. It is a fully rationalized system, the cumulation of purposively rational acts. Although it draws upon the raw materials of inconsistent rationalizations of pre-modern worlds, it resolutely sweeps them away to erect its own proud edifice on their ruins. Western music has been completely rationalized, and yet it reaches the limits of rationality very quickly. The non-rationalizable, the residual "irrational" elements within the rationalized system are "revolutionaries" or "rebels." On the one hand, they challenge the legitimacy of Occidental music; on the other, they generate a dialectical tension without which dynamic development within the system would be inconceivable. Despite its role of a dialectical stimulant, the romantic rebellion cannot pretend to transcend, let alone supersede, the rationality of the system. Insofar as the rebels find the courage or boldness, to stray beyond the limits of rationality, they can destroy the system; but they will negate it without creating anything of lasting value and significance in its stead. The Weberian strictures concerning the non-transcendability of modernity with its autonomous rationalized spheres are no less stern and no less beyond appeal here than at any other point in his system. Once the stage of 'polyvocality' was reached, the rationalized sphere of music could still continue to unfold in depth but it has nowhere left to go beyond that level.

An issue regarding this 'musical theory of action' must be addressed: at this point, where is the actor? Or more precisely: who is the actor? In fact, Weber's theory is characterized by a mysterious and almost total anonymity as far as the actor is concerned. Admittedly, this anonymity is only "almost" total, for Weber does briefly refer to the roles of "professionals," as the manufacturers of musical instruments, the priestly castes and the virtuosi. In the main, however, it is "music as such" that, in Weber's theory, unfolds and makes progress toward rationalization through acts of purposive rationality. It is "Western music" as such that had been locked into and has come victoriously out of a long struggle with its antagonist, "pre-rational music." The anonymity created by the (almost total) absence of the actor, the *sensu stricto* career of the rationalizing process, generates a quasi-natural (in Marxist vocabulary "reified") atmosphere in Weber's theory. But why this anonymity? Why a mathematical theory of the basis for musical creation without an adequate account of the musical actor?

The likeliest answer to this dilemma is that, had Weber undertaken a sociology of the actor, he could not have escaped taking up the analysis of *interspheric relations* and their causal or noncausal nature. At the same time it is clear that, although he had learned enormously from Marx, Weber was a lifelong adversary of historical materialism, with its "cause-and-effect" conception of the interspheric relations of social life. However, to refrain from taking up the all-too-obvious problem of the stunning resemblance of autonomous spheres to one another does not provide any solution to the puzzle. If the spheres are perfectly autonomous with regard to their genesis and functioning, and yet display strikingly similar structures, *praestabilita harmonia* of a kind must be behind these parallels and similarities. While this is perfectly in keeping with the *mathematica sacra* of Kepler and his passionate inquiry into the "music of the spheres," it does not sit well with the great sociologist who pleaded "religious unmusicality" and in whose work music had emerged as the yield of "this-worldly" mathematics. Perhaps at this point, the legacy and the fate of Western rationalization affected its major theorist. Strongly insistent on a fully rationalized theory, he very soon felt the limits of his own rationality.

## Adorno and Bloch: Two Representative Critics of Weber's Theory of Music

Adorno's position was linked to Weber's theory of rationalized music by closer ties, both positive and negative, than he would have been prepared to acknowledge. True to his strange habit of remaining silent about his predecessors, Adorno's anti-Weber stance in his *Philosophy of Modern Music* is only implicit, if vehement, and Weber's stimulus to Adorno's theory of music is never mentioned. Yet as a stimulus, Weber is crucial to Adorno. Many analysts have pondered the meaning of Adorno's mysterious, although repeated and quite unequivocal, statements that music is bourgeois (in the sense of *hbürgerlich*). Needless to say, taken literally, this curt verdict flies in the face not only of the fundamental facts of the history of music but also of Adorno's frequently stated admiration for Palestrina. However, if we regard Adorno as a conditional subscriber to Weber's theory of the rationalization of music, the puzzle is solved. Music is bourgeois ( *hbürgerlich*) insofar as it is fully rationalized because, and at this point Adorno is in agreement with Weber, ongoing and self-completing rationalization is the very essence of the epoch which is termed modern or bourgeois.

More important than the initial stimulus, however, is that Adorno's attack against Weber is premised on the self-consuming, negative dialectic of the Enlightenment.

Here is the fullest polemical statement from *Philosophy of Modern Music*:

The assumption of an historical tendency in musical material contradicts the traditional conception of the material of music. This material is traditionally defined . . . as the sum of all sounds at the disposal of the composer. The actual compositional material, however, is as different from this sum as is language from its total supply of sounds. It is not simply a matter of increase and decrease of this supply in the course of history. All its specific characteristics are indications of the historical process . . . Music recognizes no natural law . . . a unique ontological law is by no means to be ascribed either to the material of tones itself or to the tonal material which has been filtered through the tempered system. This, for example, is the typical argumentation of those who—either from the relationships of harmonic tones or from the psychology of the ear— attempt to deduce that the triad is the necessary and universally valid condition of all possible comprehension and that, therefore, all music must be dependent upon it. This argumentation . . . is nothing but a superstructure for reactionary compositional tendencies . . . That which seems to be the mere self-locomotion of the material is of the same origin as is the social process, by whose traces it is continually permeated.[9]

What is wrong with the theory of "mathematical self-locomotion" or the Weberian conception of the rationalization of music? The details of Adorno's argument are well known and can therefore be briefly summarized here. In the historically conditioned ongoing process of rationalization, yesterday's achievement has gradually become today's dilemma:

All the tonal combinations employed in the past by no means stand indiscriminately at the disposal of the composer today. Even the more insensitive ear detects the shabbiness and exhaustion of the diminished seventh chord and certain chromatic modulatory tones in the salon music of the nineteenth century. For the technically trained ear, such vague discomfort is transformed into a prohibitive canon . . . this canon today excludes even the medium of tonality— that is to say, the means of all traditional music. It is not simply that these sounds are antiquated and untimely, but that they are false. They no longer fulfill their function. The most progressive level of technical procedures designs tasks before which traditional sounds reveal themselves as impotent cliches. .. . . . It is precisely the triads which, in such context, are cacophonous and not the dissonances.[10]

The historical dialectic explodes the boundaries of the traditional musical world and creates a new sonorous domain of seemingly unlimited liberties:

All restricting principles of selection in tonality have been discarded. Traditional music had to content itself with a highly limited number of tonal combinations, particularly with regard to their vertical application . . . Today, in contrast . . . no conventions prevent the composer from using the sound which he needs in a specific spot. No convention forces him to acquiesce to traditionally universal principles. With the liberation of musical material, there arose the possibility of mastering it technically. It is as if music had thrown off that last alleged force of nature which its subject matter exercises upon it, and would now be able to assume command over this subject matter freely, consciously and openly. The composer has emancipated himself along with his sounds.[11]

Breaking through the barrier of traditional, quasi-natural musical conventions, i.e., rationalized music in the Weberian sense, is however, not merely liberating. For specific reasons, it also ushers in the period of rationalization of a *higher* type:

The various dimensions of Western tonal music—melody, harmony, counterpoint, form, and instrumentation—have for the most part developed historically apart from one another, without design, and, in that regard, according to the "laws of nature." . . . Melody circumscribed the harmonic function; harmony differentiated itself in the service of melodic valor. . . . In a later development a common denominator is sought for all musical dimensions. This is the origin of the twelve-tone technique, which finds its culmination in the will towards the suspension of that fundamental contrast upon which all Western music is built—the contrast between polyphonic fugal structure and homophonic sonata-form.[12]

Already the traditional-conventional music, that is, the Weberian "rationalized" phase of Occidental music had known autonomous musical subjectivity, a term with the aid of which Adorno wanted to overcome the reification of the Weberian "musical self-locomotion." However, the exact meaning of the term is not entirely clear in Adorno's text. The most likely application of the term probably covers the type of art work that has its roots in convention but which has already gained the level of the autonomous musical subject; it is best exemplified by Beethoven's sonata-form. The more the center of music is shifted from universalistic-conventional organization and rule-following towards the heroic, unique and idiosyncratic, but still rational autonomous musical subject, the more will Beethoven occupy the place of the Weberian paradigmatic figure, Bach on the peak of a musical Olympus. However, the hopes tied to this new phase of musical rationalization turned out to be short-lived:

A system by which music dominates nature results. . . . The conscious disposition over the material of nature is two-sided: the emancipation of the human being from the musical force of nature and the subjection of nature to human purposes . . . At the same time, however, this technique further approaches the ideal of mastery as domination, the infinity of which resides in the fact that nothing heteronomous remains which is not absorbed into the continuum of this technique. Infinity is pure identity. . . . Music, in its surrender to historical dialectics, has played its role in this process. Twelve-tone technique is truly the fate of music. It enchains music by liberating it. The subject dominates through the rationality of the system, only in order to succumb to the rational system itself. . . . From the procedures which broke the blind domination of tonal material there evolves a second blind nature by means of this regulatory system. . . . The total rationality of music is its total organization.[13]

The total or rather totalitarian fiasco of the second rationalization of music leaves only one of two alternative outcomes: either the abandonment of the twelve-tone system and the selection of some undefined musical path of a new freedom or the end of music.

Without doubt, Adorno's critique of Weber contains some serious injustices. The theory of Western rationalization, which at every point concluded in the disenchantment of the world, concealed and very often disclosed almost tragic tensions. In *History and Class Consciousness*, when Lukacs used Weber's own characterization of rationality in order to leave behind the whole domain of purposive rationality, he acted in a dangerous fashion against the stricture but not necessarily against the spirit of at least one of Weber's (whose soul was so thoroughly split on this matter) most profound intentions. And yet, a new theory of music has emerged from Adorno's biased polemic, in which the rationalization thesis has acquired new and deeper dimensions. Rationality here ceases to be a result of purposive actions, a result not teleological in nature. It has been plugged into the historical process whose telos, in good Hegelian fashion, is freedom. It is precisely freedom that becomes the yardstick, with which to measure rationality. Insofar as rationality becomes domination and freedom evaporates from rationalized objectivations, insofar as the first or second wave of rationalization oppresses the autonomous musical subject which could only enjoy a single historical moment of self-emancipation, rationalization becomes an oppressive trend. It turns against the intentions of the Western project. Furthermore, the dialectic of Western rationalization, a trend that Weber also detected but which he believed to have been subordinated to the general pattern of the rationalizing schema, has in Adorno been transformed into the spasmodic but grandiose cycle of an overwhelmingly negative dialectic. This transformation provides us with a deeply problematic philosophy of history. At the same time, it presents us a magnificent philosophy of Occidental music which accounts for its somber, internally split and dramatic grandeur in a way that is incomparably deeper than the Weberian thesis of "rationalizing self-locomotion."

Even less well known than Adorno's simultaneously negative and positive attachment to Weber's thesis is the fact that Ernst Bloch also began his early philosophy of music with a covert polemic against Weber's thesis and that, in this sense, Weber's theory also served for Bloch as a powerful negative stimulus. According to the testimony of his correspondence,[14] Bloch was working on "Philosophy of Music" (which became part of both the first and the final second version of *The Spirit of Utopia*) during the summer of 1915. Bloch, who never belonged to the Weber-circle and who felt enormous resentment against his omission from this intellectual paradise, could not possibly have been acquainted with Weber's essay in manuscript. However, we do know, once again from Bloch's correspondence, that he discussed the plan of "Philosophy of Music" (which had been growing in him for some years) with Weber, who proved a uniquely insensitive audience. It cannot be any accident that the single polemical motif in which Bloch captured the message of his philosophy of music, in a letter to Lukacs, was an invective against the idea of musical "progress," which was of course central to Weber's rationalization thesis.[15]

Neither prophets nor journalists write dissertations. Bloch was a mixture of both, and this is why his frontal attack on the theory of musical rationalization is so unsystematic but, also, undeniably, why it offers so many deep and unexpected insights. Bloch makes his incursion into Weber's position exactly at the point where Weber himself felt a dialectical tension to have been injected into the edifice of Western music, at the point where, later, Adorno identified the stimulus for changing the form of rationalization, namely in the tension between the constructive-rational and the affective, the harmonic and the melodic aspects of modern music. Yet Bloch's message is more profound than the mere reductive contrasting of the harmonic to the melodic. For Bloch, the whole idea of rationalizing music is yet another version of those futile attempts which aim at reforming human existence through the domain of the calculable (e.g., the economic) and which he called, in *The Spirit*

*of Utopia, die Verwaltung des Unwesentlichen*, the management
of the insignificant. Most specifically irrelevant is the term
"progress" in understanding both the history and the function of
music. There is indeed some sort of gradual improvement in the
*atelier* aspect of handling and arranging the musical material,
Bloch admits in a polemic against Lukacs (and the *spiritus rector*,
Weber). However, he reveals his intentions when he suggests a
seemingly totally paradoxical, if not outright nonsensical,
historical typology of music in which Mozart is placed lower on
the rungs of the ladder of rationalization than Bach and therefore
appears to be temporarily prior to him.

The key to the puzzle is in Bloch's "mystical-musical egology."
He contends that subjectivity, the Ego and its historical
metamorphoses, constitutes the heart and the center of music, and
not some sort of rationalized structure within the material which
either "manages the insignificant," or enchains one to one's
existence. In composing and appropriating music, one builds an
"Ego-like house" (ein ichhaftes Haus), the dimension and the
beauty of which depend on the creative and appropriating Ego.
History is a mere receptacle in which the metamorphosis of this
Ego takes place. In this neutral medium it could easily happen
that the paradigmatic figure of a lower level of this egology appears
at a historically later stage than the paradigm of a higher level.
The egological typology has four stages. First is the stage of the
"small worldly Ego," the harmonic, the Greek, the one which dwells
in perfect harmony but which is not familiar with the metaphysical
tension that drives us towards our proper destiny. Mozart is
representative of this stage with his fifteen-year-old's music. The
"small spiritual Ego" is expressed in the second stage, and is
exemplified by Bach. The house of this Ego is small, the atmosphere
that reigns supreme in it is one of devotion, piety, tacit exaltation.
But its windows open onto nowhere. Eyes turn towards the
inwardness, the sound comes from within, and the addressee is
precisely this sonorous inwardness, not any kind of external
audience. It is difficult to decide whether the hero of the third stage,
that of the "large worldly Ego" epitomized by Beethoven, Wagner,
and Bruckner, lives in a house at all. For, the "large worldly Ego"
lives in the world at large. It is a public and heroic figure. It
challenges the skies and what is beyond. The music of the Gral
or another mysterious Mana lifts up from its enlarged orchestra.
Finally, the fourth stage, that of the "large spiritual Ego" has
not yet come. There have been certain forerunners of the "large

spiritual Ego" but Sigfried turned out to be the false Messiah. We still have to wait.[17]

There are two possible readings of Bloch's philosophy of music which are equally true but not of the same breadth, scope, and depth. In terms of the first, his polemic against the rationalization thesis, his emphasis on the affective element of music presents the best theoretical anticipation of and preparation for musical Expressionism in the pre-World War I era. This historical and therefore somewhat reductive interpretation has many supporting arguments, the most important of which is Bloch's attitude. In turning back to the Kierkegaardian parable of the poet who is slowly burning to death in the interior of the iron bull where he had been thrown by the tyrant in wrath, and who imperturbably chants his swansong, Bloch indignantly asks the "rationalizers": what are we looking for in listening to this song? Is it the well-arranged melismas of the song that capture our attention or the brutal message of his suffering, everyone's suffering, that makes us "richer" for listening?[18] This untarnished advocacy of an Expressionist *Inhaltsästhetik* becomes even more explicit when Bloch turns against "musical number-crunching" and when, significantly, he makes the criticism against Schönberg's imminent turn towards dodecaphony, which he brilliantly anticipates, that the answer to the dilemma of music cannot be found in further mathematization, only in freer, "larger" expressivity.[19]

The second reading of Bloch's theory is mystical-eschatological. The fourth stage of the egological typology will only be realized simultaneously with parousia. It is not by chance that, when he is explicit about his intentions, Bloch reaches back to Kierkegaard. Admittedly, his reading of Kierkegaard is fairly arbitrary because the sphere of the religious in Kierkegaard comes long after he had left the sphere of the aesthetic whereas with Bloch, music is the antechamber of parousia. Yet once the music of the fourth stage resounds, all Egos are on the threshold of their imminent unification with that infinite transcendental subject. If we translate Bloch's position again, however, and those without faith perforce translate, we come to a surprising revelation. We shall perceive that, in fact, the music of the third stage, the music of the Ninth Symphony, implicitly contains the music of the fourth stage, that of the large spiritual Ego. Parousia can also mean " the end of prehistory" (a shade of meaning embraced later by Ernst Bloch himself). The Mana whose sounds we perceive can usher us into the unification ceremony with the ultimate transcendental Ego, but it can also announce the moment of *seid umschlungen, Millionen*, the festivity of the Supreme Being, humankind's (or the World Spirit's) homecoming, an end to the vicissitudes of history. If we read Bloch's text in this second sense, we shall view music as the peak of the rationalist project of the Enlightenment even after the repeated collapse of attempts at its mathematical—"technological" rationalization. *For then, music alone will appear as the appropriate abode of the concept "humankind,"* which is the precondition and the ultimate justification of rationalism in the same measure. Occidental music will thus appear as the only shelter in which rationalism can survive the periods of persecution and critical questioning to which it has no properly rational answers.

What do we do when, in the spirit of Beethoven, we hug millions? We certainly do not make love. Humankind does not have an erotic, hardly even an affective emanation. Caught red-handed by Heidegger at the old-fashioned sin of humanism, it was still Sartre who rightly questioned the possibility of "being fond of humanity." Nor are we engaged in political action when we listen to music and hug millions. Both Plato and Thomas Mann were right in regarding music as politically suspect. While under its spell, we are more indeterminate and unspecific in our hates and sympathies than politics would like us to be. There is no doubt that we communicate while we are listening to music and hugging millions. But this is a special kind of communication. Its message is meager yet redundant. It conveys to those millions in my embrace only the truism that they are like me and I am like them. It is a discourse that knows no argument; indeed it is one that draws its strength from the absence of argument. Whenever conceptual issues, such as human rights or economic world systems, are on the agenda of the discourse of humanism, the overarching or underlying term, humankind, suffers more defeats than it heralds victories. Not so in music when we do not bring up argument against argument but we prove, by the very fact that we are absorbed and enchanted by the mana of music together with those we hug and by whom we are being hugged, that we are the same species. In this sense, music is indeed communication; together with mathematics, it is the only universal language. This is perhaps the greatest vindication of the rationality of music. It is also the reason why, once attempts are made (e.g., by Adrian Leverkühn) at revoking the Ninth Symphony, the very project of Occidental music is destroyed.

## Reference Notes

1. Max Weber 1958. *The Rational and Social Foundations of Music.* Translated by D. Martindale, J. Riedel, G Neuwirth. Southern Illinois University Press. The Introduction, which I refer to extensively in describing Weber's theory, is the work of D. Martindale and J. Riedel.
2. Weber, op. cit., Introduction, p. xxii
3. Weber, op. cit., pp. 3–6.
4. Weber, op. cit., Introduction, p. xxxvi.
5. Weber, op. cit. pp. 6–7 (emphasis mine). It is perhaps more than accidental that the melancholy report on the impossibility of fully rationalizing music on the basis of mathematical principles is roughly coequal with the other spectacular admission of the limits to Western rationality, namely with Russell's resignation. *Principia Mathematica*, too, had to be ended on a note of resignation; mathematics could not be fully based on logical principles.
6. Weber, op. cit. pp. 8–10 (emphasis mine). It is noteworthy that again, the "scale-alien tones" that generate melody and which from the viewpoint of chord aesthetics are resistent alien bodies, are called "rebels" by Weber.
7. Weber, op. cit. Introduction, pp. xxxvii–xxxviii.
8. Weber, op. cit., p. 102. (my emphasis)
9. Theodor W. Adorno 1983. *Philosophy of Modern Music.* Translated by Anne G. Mitchell and Wesley V. Blomster. New York: The Seabury Press, pp. 32–33.
10. Adorno, op. cit., p. 34.
11. Adorno, op. cit., pp. 51–52. A very good and convincing description of the (negative) dialectic of "musical self-emancipation," in Adorno's theory; can be found in David Roberts' *After Adorno: Towards a Theory of Post-Modern Art.* A totally false conception of the "rationalization as emancipation" of music appeared on the left roughly at the same time. It hailed the "Tailorization of music," which allegedly contained the possibility for the "radicalization of evil:" in undermining the traditional forms of performing music, a new era would be ushered in, in which there would be no difference between composer and listener, performer and audience. Here is the most aggressive statement of this idea, made by Hans Eisler, which was admired by Walter Benjamin: "In the development of music, too, both in production and in reproduction, we must learn to perceive an ever increasing process of rationalization . . . The gramophone record, the sound film, jukeboxes can purvey top quality music . . . canned as commodity. The consequence of this process of rationalization is that musical reproduction is consigned to ever diminishing, but also ever more highly qualified, groups of specialists. The crisis of commercial concert is the crisis of an antiquated form of production made obsolete by new technical inventions." Quoted in W. Benjamin, "The Author as Producer," in Arato-Gebhardt, *The Frankfurt School Reader*, p. 263.
12. Ibid., 53–54.
13. Ibid., 65–69.
14. Ernst Bloch 1983, *Briefe 1903–1975*, vol. 1. Frankfurt: Suhrkamp, p. 157.
15. Op. cit., 160.
16. Ernst Bloch *Der Geist der Utopie*, Erste Fassung, Frankfurt: Suhrkamp Verlag, 177.
17. Bloch, op. cit., 211–212.
18. Bloch, op. cit., 178.
19. Ibid., 189–190.

# About the Authors

**Judith H. Balfe's** current research focuses on the institutionalization of art. Her publications include *Art, Ideology and Politics*, and articles in *New Literary History* and the *Journal Of Arts, Management And Law*. She is Assistant Professor of Sociology, College of Staten Island, C. U. N. Y., Staten Island, N. Y. 10301.

**Larry S. Carney** teaches sociology at Rhode Island College. He is co-author of *Women and Men in Society: Crosscultural Perspectives in Gender Stratification* and the forthcoming *Captives of Affluence: Women's Place in Modern Japan*. Mailing address: 76 Summit Avenue, Providence, R. I. 02906.

**Ferenc Feher's** publications include *The Frozen Revolution* and *Dostoevsky and the Crisis of the Individual*. He is coauthor of *Dictatorship Over Needs, Eastern Left—Western Left, Reconstructing Aesthetics*, and *Doomsday or Deterrence*. He is teaching Aesthetics at the New School for Social Research in the Liberal Studies Department, 65 Fifth Avenue, New York, NY 10003.

**Robert Lilienfeld** has worked with the late Joseph Bensman on a number of projects, including *Craft and Consciousness*, soon to appear in its second edition, with new chapters. He has also published on *The Rise of Systems Theory*, and is presently at work on the current crisis of sociology. He is a professor in the Department of Sociology at the City University of New York, New York, N. Y. 10031.

**Stanford M. Lyman** is author of *Chinatown and Little Tokyo: Power, Conflict, and Community Among Chinese and Japanese Immigrants in America*, and *American Sociology: Worldly Rejections of Religions and Their Directions* (with Arthur J. Vidich). His forthcoming work is *Social Order and the Public Philosophy: An Analysis and Interpretation of the Work of Herbert Blumer*, co-authored with Arthur J. Vidich. He is Robert J. Morrow Eminent Scholar and Professor of Social Science, Florida Atlantic University, P. O. Box 3091, Boca Raton, Florida 33431-0991.

**Dimitri Monos** is author of *The Achievements of the Greeks in the U. S.* and *A Manual for Conducting Research in Community*

*History*. He is Associate Professor of Sociology, Department of Sociology—OLB, West Chester University, West Chester, PA, 19383.

**Aurelio Orensanz** is a Lecturer at the New School's School of Management and Urban Professions and is engaged in research on urban ethnic communities in the U. S. His publications include *Presentations of Art in Society, Revolution Elsewhere, Anarchy and Christianity*. Mailing address: 193 Tenth Avenue, New York, N. Y. 10011.

**Charles R. Simpson's** research interests include the sociology of arts and community. He is author of *SoHo: The Artist in the City*. His articles on culture include "Popular Culture as Civil Religion: The Collective Imagination and the Social Integration of Mass Society" and "Community as a Relief from History: Thornton Wilder's *Our Town*." He is Associate Professor of Sociology at SUNY/Plattsburgh, N. Y. 12901.

All inquiries concerning essays published in this journal should be made directly to their authors unless otherwise noted.

STATEMENT OF OWNERSHIP MANAGEMENT AND CIRCULATION

International Journal of Politics, Culture & Society

Quarterly

Human Sciences Press, 72 Fifth Avenue, New York, NY 10011-8004

Sheldon Rovin, Human Sciences Press, 72 Fifth Avenue, New York, NY 10011-8004

Arthur Vidich, New School for Social Research, 65 Fifth Avenue, New York, NY 10003

Christopher Daly, Human Sciences Press, 72 Fifth Avenue, New York, NY 10011-8004

Human Sciences Press — 72 Fifth Avenue, New York, NY 10011